DISCARD

WIN

—THE—

CUSTOMER

70 SIMPLE RULES FOR SENSATIONAL SERVICE

FLAVIO MARTINS

◢AMACOM

American Management Association

New York • Atlanta • Brussels • Chicago • Mexico City • San Francisco
Shanghai • Tokyo • Toronto • Washington, D.C.

Bulk discounts available. For details visit:
www.amacombooks.org/go/specialsales
Or contact special sales:
Phone: 800-250-5308
Email: specialsls@amanet.org
View all the AMACOM titles at: www.amacombooks.org
American Management Association: www.amanet.org

This publication is designed to provide accurate and authoritative information in regard to the subject matter covered. It is sold with the understanding that the publisher is not engaged in rendering legal, accounting, or other professional service. If legal advice or other expert assistance is required, the services of a competent professional person should be sought.

Library of Congress Cataloging-in-Publication Data

Martins, Flavio.
   Win the customer : 70 simple rules for sensational service / Flavio Martins.
     pages cm
   Includes index.
   ISBN 978-0-8144-3624-0 (hardcover) — ISBN 978-0-8144-3625-7 (ebook) 1. Customer services. 2. Consumer satisfaction. 3. Customer relations. I. Title.
   HF5415.5.M173 2015
   658.8'12—dc23
                                      2015012548

ABOUT AMA
American Management Association (www.amanet.org) is a world leader in talent development, advancing the skills of individuals to drive business success. Our mission is to support the goals of individuals and organizations through a complete range of products and services, including classroom and virtual seminars, webcasts, webinars, podcasts, conferences, corporate and government solutions, business books, and research. AMA's approach to improving performance combines experiential learning—learning through doing—with opportunities for ongoing professional growth at every step of one's career journey.

Printing number

10 9 8 7 6 5 4 3 2 1

To Niki, who took a chance on me.
May you truly live happily ever after.

Contents

Introduction

In today's competitive business world, most businesses inevitably will face the commoditization of their products or services. How, then, can they distinguish themselves from the dozens of nearly identical competitor products and services? In the absence of a reason, it's often said, customers will choose price. But what if your business can give its customers something special, something that can't be duplicated, whatever the price? What if you can offer something unique that no other competitor can provide? You can do this by delivering a winning customer service experience.

There are many good reasons why you should have outstanding customer service. You've probably already seen that your loyal customers, those who are emotionally attached to your business, will spend more than those who are not connected to you, who think your service is just OK. Offering excellent customer service that consistently delivers results that leave customers more than just "satisfied" is critical to the long-term growth of your organization. Loyal customers will promote your excellent service by word of mouth to friends, family, colleagues, and coworkers. Loyal customers also tend to spend considerably more than new customers. And keeping existing customers happy costs considerably less than attracting new ones.

Companies recognized for their exceptional customer service know that to achieve effective service success and great customer satisfaction ratings, it's important that employees understand the customer's needs and are empowered to make decisions for themselves. Employees need to be imaginative in order to be able to act decisively, yet innovatively, and have the personality required to deliver a unique style of service. Customer service has to be delivered in a welcoming, positive atmosphere; the employees must be approachable, have excellent interaction skills, and be enthusiastic to help customers. This will ensure that they have the ability to offer timely solutions to any given problems.

Organizations and individuals who want to take their customer relationships to the next level need to focus on customer-care effectiveness and develop their customer-care core principles in a way that can be maintained and improved on an ongoing basis. In these difficult economic times, you can take your chances with an average customer service program and eventually fall by the wayside or you can choose to deliver exceptional customer service and reap the rewards of deserved reputation and increased profitability, as well as improved workplace morale. Winning long-term customer loyalty is what this is all about; exceptional, memorable experiences are what bond customers emotionally to your business.

By aligning everyone in your organization around a customer service mission and developing day-to-day actions based on the values of customer service, you can ensure that your people will do and say the right thing to develop the type of relationship with your customers that will turn them into lifelong fans.

Unfortunately, customer service books come in just a few flavors. Some focus on "exceptional customer service" stories that show the lengths to which some organizations will go for service but that aren't often applicable in day-to-day service work. Others emphasize overly simplified games or role-playing situations to be performed (almost always awkwardly) in training meetings. Finally, there are books saturated with jargon that dive too deep into statistics and theoretical discussions about the psychology of selling to customers, but leave few practical takeaways for those looking to refresh their approach to working with customers.

The 70 service rules I present in *Win the Customer* can be used as a top-down resource in organizations looking to develop or enhance a service culture. They can also be used as a resource for individuals who want to transform the way service is handled from the ground up, even when lacking the full commitment and support from organization-wide training and change efforts. The rules are laid out in short sections with inspirational insight that can be applied in corporations, startups, nonprofits, small businesses, educational organizations, and government agencies.

▶ Executives can use the book as inspiration for their future management decisions, as well as to help their organizations catch that special vision of what it means to deliver exceptional service experiences.

▶ Managers in medium-size and large organizations can use it to gauge their effectiveness in getting their frontline employees to create a better customer service experience.

▶ Small-business owners can use it as their go-to manual for how to create a service culture and make what they do stand out against the competition.

▶ Frontline employees can use it as practical advice for the typical customer service circumstances they face, as well as to maintain a great customer service frame of mind.

Every customer is an opportunity. Every single customer counts. Remember this every time you interact with a customer and it will motivate positive action in the service experience. Customers aren't perfect. They can be unreasonable in their demands and expectations. They lie or leave out important details, they break things and don't admit it, they don't take the time to do things right, and they almost never read instructions. They rarely use words and phrases in the best way to assist in the service process. But if you choose to overcome and look past the faults of the customer, continuing to seek opportunities to go above and beyond, you're more likely to have customers who recognize your efforts and appreciate your willingness to serve them. The customer is not always right, but wrong customers are still customers.

The service rules discussed in this book can be used as a standard by which individuals and organizations can measure the effectiveness of their processes of serving customers and creating a customer-focused culture. The rules can also be used as references for effective, straightforward, results-oriented instructions for engaging with customers on a more personal level and to deliver the type of actions that wins customer loyalty time and time again.

Rule 1

BE PREPARED TO BREAK TRADITIONAL RULES

▶ For a book all about rules to begin by suggesting that the rules should be broken seems somewhat ironic, doesn't it? The idea of breaking rules isn't that you literally should break every rule of thumb, but only that you should constantly evaluate every established rule or operating practice for its effectiveness and measure its ultimate result. The rules should become rules only as they are proven through their real effect and final results. No, we're not talking about doing anything illegal, unethical, or immoral. Some traditional rules are perfectly fine and should remain constants as you do business, but what we've come to know as best practices and rules of thumb should be reevaluated to ensure that they really deliver the results you want.

The one-size-fits-all theory of customer service is futile in today's world. Achieving consistently excellent customer service nowadays requires you to learn to tell your own story; step back and ask yourself what you have to offer and what you want to achieve; learn to say no to the traditional expectations of service; and learn that you have the courage to take the first step toward change and the resilience to stick with what your gut tells you is the right approach, even when others may say it's foolishness. Instead of constantly struggling to keep business and customer interests in balance, give up this eternal struggle and forge a new path by uniting your organization around interests that are good for your business and your customers.

Customer service in the modern age has become stale due to too many copy and paste service strategies. It's too much doing what others have done, and not enough boldly finding your own way to serve customers. Customers are fed up and frustrated. Except on rare occasions, customer service is just one disappointment after another. Too many businesses today run around copying each other, thinking they are doing things a bit better, when in fact there seems to be a disconnect between customer service policies and the customers a business serves. Don't think you're guilty of this? In today's competitive business landscape, organizations are falling all over themselves to try to attract and keep customers. They're using advertising, promotions, gifts, word of mouth, coupons, social media, and pretty much any avenue available in an effort to build a larger customer base.

For all of their efforts, however well-meaning and done with the best of intentions, too many organizations today ultimately miss the goal of engaging with customers in a positive and meaningful way that actually matters to them. No matter how enticing your offer may be, the truly great brands and organizations with massive customer loyalty know that something more is needed in order to really matter in the eyes of the customer. Without that level of connection, your organization will ultimately be stuck in the perpetual downward spiral of offering lower prices, while gaining equally lower customer loyalty and immensely larger customer acquisition costs.

Ask yourself, does your business route phone calls through a machine? Do you even include a phone number on your website? Is your contact information buried on some obscure page on your website? Do you force people to register online before they're able to connect with another human being? Do you have strict policies that seem to put your company goal above the needs of the customer when push comes to shove? Any of these practices—and more—are standard in many businesses. If you want to move beyond the stagnation of the average business, then it's time to break the rules of customer service.

FOCUS ON MAKING IT RIGHT

The reality is that customer service is hardly black-and-white. You have protocols, and those are good to have, but what do you do when a prospect or customer doesn't quite fit into a category? What happens when a problem isn't ordinary? What most businesses do, rather than shift their approach to helping the customer, is cram the customer into a predetermined category, hoping that what they've done will resolve the customer's issue to some degree.

On top of this, if customers aren't happy with how things were handled, they're usually fed cheap lines like, "We're sorry, sir, but there's nothing we can do," or, "It's company policy to *not* X, Y, or Z." The customer is *not* always right, but a customer is *always* a customer. Sometimes customer requests are unreasonable, but positioning your business in a way that will rise to the challenge and meet the customer's needs as best as you possibly can will determine whether you're a flourishing business or just another stopping point on the way to finding the next service provider.

BREAKING THE MOLD

So, what kind of experience do you ultimately want? Are you another "We apologize, but . . ." operation? Or are you a paragon of customer service excellence that handles your customers with respect, dignity, and generosity? The choice is entirely up to you. If you're in this for the long term, then actually start thinking long-term. Yes, some people are difficult, some customers are rude, and sometimes nothing will make the truly unreasonable customers happy. This doesn't mean you should justify handling customers like so many of the other companies out there do. Most people can be helped, so try to help them. It's time to be different, because you can impress and surprise your customers by going the extra mile for them. If it means brightening your customer's day, break the rules sometimes.

If you're ready to really engage with customers and change them from thinking of your organization as little more than an afterthought, serving customers and crafting an exceptional experience are the blueprints to getting there. Taking service to the next level means tapping into the secret source of value that comes from truly listening, comprehending, and delivering the physical, emotional, and digital needs of customers today. Professionals who know how to engage and effectively serve customers outperform their peers. Organizations that know how to engage and effectively serve the needs of their customers outperform their competition.

Staying ahead today means reevaluating every rule, every process, every metric, and every decision to ensure that it's directly contributing toward your vision of connecting with and serving customers. Otherwise, you're stuck giving the same mediocre service that everyone else gives and you'll have to be content dealing with the constant plague of unloyal customers that everyone else does.

Rule 2

CREATE THE RIGHT CULTURE FOR SERVICE

▶ Every organization has a culture, but not all cultures are effective at driving the positive results that the organization ultimately wants. Corporations, nonprofits, government entities, schools, and religious institutions have cultures. Even gangs have cultures. Some cultures are more positive than others. Employees and customers experience your customer service culture in different ways, and it's the complex nature of culture that actually drives its power in transforming and inspiring people. One reason organizational culture does not make the priority list of most leaders is that it is hard to define. But developing the internal culture of your organization will have a critical impact on the way people carry out the overall vision of your customer service.

Culture isn't sushi. Culture isn't ping-pong tables. It's not team lunches or team activities. It's the vision, values, and behaviors that the individuals in organizations share that are the governing standard by which the organization will judge its members.

> *It's really the people that make Google the kind of company it is. We hire people who are smart and determined, and we favor ability over experience. Although Googlers share common goals and visions for the company, we hail from all walks of life and speak dozens of languages, reflecting the global audience that we serve.*
> —GOOGLE CORPORATE CULTURE[1]

Culture is squishy. It's complex. Sometimes culture is even contradictory. With all the other challenges your business faces, it's easy to see why culture takes a backseat. However, success today is often directly dependent on the people within the organization. It's their passion, dedication, skill, talents, and commitment to their cause that ultimately carry them through the challenges that every organization faces and allow them to capitalize on opportunities and achieve success.

In his service e-book, *Culture That Works: How Getting Serious About Culture Unlocks New Performance*, Jamie Notter sheds light on the often-misunderstood nature of culture. Notter says, "Organizational culture is the collection of words, actions, thoughts, and 'stuff' that clarifies and reinforces what a company truly values."[2] Look at those organizations that seem to get culture right. Culture is the behaviors, norms, thoughts, and actions expected of the members of your organization. It's what you hope people will aspire to be and the way they carry out those aspirations.

CAN YOU RECOGNIZE A CUSTOMER SERVICE CULTURE? DO YOU HAVE ONE?

Many companies have a lengthy mission statement, but little of it is translated into everyday thoughts, words, and actions exhibited by the individuals in the organization. Most organizations claim to deliver good customer service or at least aspire to wow customers with their customer experience, but then go about doing the same thing that has been done in the past or that everyone else in the industry is doing, things that customers have expressed time and time again are not what they want. Having aspirations is not enough. Making declarations is meaningless. Going through the motions without the direction is wasteful.

Creating a *customer service culture* requires much more than simply saying that you have one. You have to connect thoughts, words, and deeds. Building a service culture requires clearly defining, developing, and delivering on that vision. It's in the actual doing of these things that your organization's culture will be established. A customer service culture isn't what you claim to be; it's what you are.

So, now I'll ask you to think about your culture. Take time out for a customer service culture assessment. Think about the words, thoughts, processes, rules, actions, and all of your organization's decisions and practices. Then evaluate them against what you truly want it to be. Does your customer service culture training cover the right material needed to clearly establish your culture to your organization? Would your customers agree that your customer service culture and mission are carried out in your words, thoughts, and actions? Can you clearly identify the right patterns and behaviors that individuals should follow to fit that ideal culture? Are you hiring based on people's ability to connect with and fit that mold? Does your culture clearly define the right outcomes to be expected from the actions performed by the people in your organization? Does your culture focus on the innate strengths of your people? Does your culture fit and support your vision for what you ultimately want your people and your customers to think and feel after interacting with your organization?

DEFINING THE RIGHT CULTURE

Creating the right culture is more than just selecting your office space, the type of computers you use, where you eat, or how often you have parties and social gatherings. Your culture largely depends on the type of people you enlist and the connection they create with others to support your cause.

The Right Culture Inspires

Culture isn't a mission statement; it's a statement of action. Culture isn't just an ideal you want to strive for, but the shared values, behaviors, and the proof that your actions support your ideals.

The Right Culture Fosters

When united in a common goal, people contribute to an environment where everybody willingly comes to work each day and pours their best efforts into doing what they believe will make the greatest difference.

The Right Culture Transforms

When working toward a higher purpose, the right culture has a real, positive effect on the work that is performed. It's expressed in the work with customers, the interaction between colleagues, the relationships that are established, and the connection to the ultimate purpose of the group.

Customers today crave that sense of connectedness to the people with whom they do business. In previous generations, it was easier to know who you were dealing with because you did business with the owner in your local community. Too many corporations today hide behind a faceless corporate image. Are you crafting a sterile and soulless corporate voice to communicate with customers because it seems like the professional thing to do given your company size?

STALE IS EASY; BLAND IS CHEAP

Customers today are smarter than that. They see right through it. They may not tell you, but the more stale the interaction, the less connection customers have with your organization the next time they have to make a product decision. A customer service culture is more than answering phones and replying to emails. It's more than answering questions and doing things for customers. Real customer service is connecting people with products and services that improve work and life. Great organizations and great cultures depend on great people. To attract great people, you have to invest in the frameworks to support them and then enable your people to go out and be great.

Your customers and the employees who serve them all experience your customer service culture in different ways. That complex nature of culture is what actually drives its power in transforming the customer relationship and inspiring people to go above and beyond in their service actions.

Rule 3

LEARN HOW TO UPDATE
YOUR CUSTOMER

▶ Too often, excellent customer service is seen as just doing whatever the customer asks. It isn't. You won't always be able to give your customers everything they want whenever they want it. (Remember, the customer is *not* always right.) Some books will tell you to just do it; give the customers what they want; just make it happen—whatever they want. That's not realistic. You know it and I know it. But just because you can't do it, or because something won't happen right away, doesn't excuse you from continuing to build the customer service experience. Even in those moments when the customer is on hold or waiting for what is being worked on, customer service is still happening. Keeping your customers up-to-date on the events taking place is critical to ensuring that an exceptional experience happens even when customers can't get instant service.

Every organization can have exceptional customer service, even those working with the most complex customer processes, if they can provide effective status updates to the customer. (As you go through the following points, think of banks, mortgage companies, airlines, telecoms, and other service companies with traditionally bad customer service reputations.)

THE NEED FOR USEFUL, SPECIFIC
STATUS UPDATES

Customers want to be able to track the status of their process/service/product. They want to be able to get an update on that item when they contact your organization. Think about it: Have you ever had someone complain because you were too specific in your communication? Were any customers ever upset because you gave them too much information?

In a *Harvard Business Review* article, Scott Edinger points out that effective communication can be broken down to three specific components: credibility, emotion, and logic.[1] This approach creates the base for building customer relationships and the foundation of positive customer experiences. Being credible with customers means having an understanding and background of the customer and the customer's concern. Giving status updates that take into consideration background information about the customer meets one of the essential criteria for positive communication.

Emotion in communication means connecting with customers on a personal level, with language that invokes feeling and concern for the individual receiving the message. Finally, logic addresses the need for actionable, strategic, problem-solving information. As you carefully consider the makeup of your status updates, evaluate them carefully to ensure that they meet these essential elements in order to effectively deliver an experience that turns into positive results for the customer.

GOOD STATUS UPDATES

Customized Update

"Thanks for contacting me! Your item X just left our warehouse and has checked into the processing facility. It should be there in Y days."

Specific Update

"Thanks for calling/emailing! It looks like we're at step 2 of 4 of your order for X. The final steps normally take two to four hours, and then it should be ready."

Quality Update

"Thanks for checking! Our X team is reviewing that right

now, and they normally finish processing it by the end of the day. If they run into any issues, you'll get a phone call."

BAD "STATUS UPDATES"

(Notice the quotation marks around Status Updates, since these examples aren't really statuses, nor are they real updates.)

Generic Update

"Thank you for your inquiry. Orders are normally processed in 24 to 72 hours."

Nonspecific Update

"Thank you. Someone will be in touch shortly."

Not a Real Update

"Our X team is reviewing that. I don't know when it will be done."

Getting and providing effective status updates to provide excellent customer service is based on *caring about the customer*. Always ask yourself if your process is making the customer happy, or if it is frustrating the customer. Customers want to be kept in the loop. Every customer makes an investment with you. Whether it's money, time, emotion, goods, or services, customers always make some type of investment with the organization. Customers want to know that their investment will pay off for them.

Rule 4

SERVE PEOPLE, NOT SHAREHOLDERS

Shareholders definitely have their place in business and industry. Because they can help a company advance very quickly, they should see a return on their good-faith investment in an organization. At the same time, it's important to remember that the reason most shareholders invest in a company is because of how it does business, and a major part of that is how a business handles its customers.

Too many organizations today serve the almighty shareholder, yet discount the fact that customers are what sustain a business in the long run. Losing sight of that is a bit like losing the forest for the trees. Some business owners and executives forget that it wasn't just shareholders but also the customers who have built their company from the ground up. Successful organizations have to avoid the trap of chasing short-term earnings at the expense of long-term value, instituting processes that harm employees, and making policies that take advantage of customers.

ABANDON SHAREHOLDER VALUE

Jack Welch, former CEO of General Electric, calls shareholder value *"the dumbest idea in the world."*[1] Know what to focus on. To get maximum returns, you don't focus on shareholder value as an outcome, but as a result of your actions and the direction in which you're taking your business. The bottom line is important, yes, but to obsess over money and do anything to try to squeeze a few extra dollars out of your customers—for your own sake or for the sake of your shareholders—is setting yourself up for future failure with your customers.

KEEP YOUR EYE ON THE PRIZE

In India, the term *Gandhian innovation* is often associated with "frugal innovation" or "inclusive innovation."[2] I like to think that it also includes the idea of holistic innovation and is the way forward in the changing tides of developing separation from competitors through differing experiences. Emphasizing customer focus can be a powerful source of unity within any organization, much more powerful than emphasis on stock price or profit for shareholders.

At Walmart, posted on a wall near the customer service desk is a sign showing the current value of the Walmart stock. Underneath the stock price reads the inscription, "Tomorrow depends on you." Do the employees really believe that their actions impact the overall results within the organization? Is displaying a financial goal an effective motivator of positive customer agent action? Or is the more appropriate question, "How many of the employees at that Walmart even own a share of Walmart stock?"

Shareholder value, stock price, and revenue goals are often too abstract as concepts and disconnected from the life of the frontline service agent to impact the individual customer interaction. The financial results can be the byproducts of getting the experience right, but they rarely are effective at driving innovation in customer experience.

Harmons, a Utah-based grocery store chain, has legendary status when it comes to the shopping experience. Brothers Bob and Randy Harmon, grandsons of the original founders, Jake and Irene Harmon, have reinvented the concept of the grocery store, moving away from the big-box model and focusing instead on educating customers on the value of fresh, quality items and caring food experts. The Harmons approach emphasizes more employees making handcrafted foods and educating shoppers. From its daily delivered and shelved produce items to fresh breads made from scratch each day, Harmons partners with growers and food producers to reduce the time from crop to shop.[3]

While smaller in terms of revenue and supply chain compared with Walmart, Harmons customers are fiercely loyal about the food experience they receive from shopping at Harmons. Employees are rewarded as each store reaches its customer experience goals. The mission statement of the organization, "Value our associates, exceed the customers' expectations," comes through from the moment you step into one of the stores to the experience you have while checking out with a friendly cashier.

Stop trying to simply copy what other organizations are doing and get to the heart of what your customers really want. Then invest in those people who have the talents, skills, and abilities to meet those customer expectations and get out of the way so they can do what they do best.

PUT THE RIGHT PEOPLE IN THE RIGHT PLACE AT THE RIGHT TIME DOING THE RIGHT THING

▶ Running a successful business is much the same as running a well-oiled machine. For a machine to run at its maximum potential, it must consist of top-quality parts and receive efficient and regular maintenance. Customer service is exactly the same: The most important parts of the customer service machine are its people, and maintenance of customer service entails employing the right people for the right positions, ensuring they have in-depth training, providing them with the right tools for the job, and treating them as the vital and important people they are.

To achieve excellent customer service, there's so much more involved than just saying the words. So many businesses, both large and small, deliver mundane and stale customer service because hiring personnel in customer service is such an ever-changing scene. Why not up the ante and start playing a different customer service game? It's the only way to win!

CHANGE YOUR IDEAS ABOUT CUSTOMER SERVICE

You need to change your ideas about customer service because there's so much at stake. Instead of thinking of customer service in the same old way, why not decide to reevaluate your interpretation of the right person for the job? Change what qualifies as the right amount of experience for your customer service position. Reconsider your view on what's the right fit for your team and perhaps change it to what's the right fit for your customers. Your customer service personnel represent you and your business, so when you're choosing people for employment in your business, hire them for their good-natured personalities and their talent in working with people, not for their previous work experience.

BE CLEAR ABOUT YOUR EXPECTATIONS

Set specific expectations for your service staff and be clear about the outcomes you expect from the relationship between your staff and your customers. Certainly, most staff members know their job, but do they really understand just how important excellent customer service is? Motivate and encourage your staff members by focusing on their own specific strengths. To develop a talented team, take more time when hiring staff to find the perfect fit for each person's skills and abilities.

Your customer service agents need a support structure, as do your team leaders, your service managers, and service executives. Customer service as a whole is a process in itself. You must teach people how to interact with customers, learn from their failures, and consistently improve on customer service expectations. This is the only way to build a high-performing service team.

EVERYONE IN YOUR ORGANIZATION
IS A CUSTOMER SERVICE AGENT

Customer service is a very personal human interaction, and these interactions are occurring in your business and with your customers all the time. In some way, shape, or form every staff member contributes to a customer's overall experience. Certainly not every staff member works directly with customers. However, your support people, such as the accounting department, cleaning staff, developers, and so on, all do something that affects those who serve customers or something that affects customers themselves. Every single staff member affects your brand, and each person should be willing and able to assist customers in an efficient, professional, and friendly manner when interacting with them.

Regardless of whether they're working directly with your customers on a day-to-day basis, or how staff members conduct themselves outside their working day, people do notice, and it definitely reflects on your brand's image. You may believe that the guys in the IT department or the shelf-stackers don't need any customer service skills, but you're wrong. They absolutely do! Every person in your employ can affect a potential customer, somehow, on some level. Never neglect the importance of excellent customer service skills and always remember how vital it is that each and every customer has an exceptional experience when conducting business with your organization.

Of course, it's also important that all your staff members work well together. There may be many people qualified to fulfill a certain position in your organization. However, if they're unfriendly or rude, this will affect the whole work atmosphere and the morale of your staff. Being good at what they do is not enough. There's a lot more to being successful in business than just being good at what you do. Each and every person in your employ must understand that they represent your company and your brand, and they should do this by offering every customer an exceptional experience.

WORK TOGETHER AS A TEAM

Every customer service agent must be loyal to your business and must be prepared to deliver powerful and consistently high customer service experiences. Unfortunately, today's customers have learned not to expect very much in the way of customer service, but you can use this fact to your advantage. This is your opportunity. All customers would love to receive great service, but they certainly don't expect it. It's exceptional customer service that makes people loyal to a business or brand. You can make this happen by ensuring that every staff member is on board with what you're trying to achieve.

SOMETIMES, EXPERIENCE IS NOT WHAT YOU NEED

A lot of businesses looking for people to hire for customer service positions insist on hiring applicants with a few years' experience in a similar industry. It's a pity that they demand such extensive experience, because in doing so they're alienating many applicants who could potentially be fantastic employees. Excellent customer service and good workplace dynamics all boil down to personalities. If customer service agents aren't already set in their ways, it doesn't take long to train them to your high standards, so perhaps this might be a better approach to hiring your customer service staff.

Too many organizations become so obsessed with the bottom line that they lose sight of the overall picture. A Bain & Company service delivery report showed that an astonishing 80 percent of businesses believed they delivered a superior customer service experience, while only 8 percent of their customers agreed that those same companies delivered a superior service experience. What's worse, when Bain surveyed the management team in those organizations, 95 percent of them believed that they were customer focused.[1] Don't cut corners. Hire the right people, train them the right way, give them one voice—your business voice—and watch your company grow.

Rule 6

LEARN SOMETHING NEW EVERY DAY

Don't you love when recent college grads with a customer service major apply for a position with your organization? OK, that's a trick question—colleges don't really have customer service majors, let alone a single customer service class. Harvard has a renowned class on negotiation and conflict resolution, and there are classes for both social psychology and clinical psychology, but why not have classes dedicated to customer service? There are some crazy college courses out there: Harry Potter: Literary Tradition and Popular Culture (Otis College); Philosophy and *Star Trek* (Georgetown University); Tattoos in American Pop Culture (Pitzer College); Lady Gaga and the Sociology of Fame (University of South Carolina–Columbia); and even The Art of Walking (Centre College)! Seriously now, walking! And you're telling me customer service can't get a course in college today? When did customer service become so uncool that it can't even compete with something as simple as walking?

For whatever reason, most people just aren't yet prepared or in a state of mind to understand customer service. It's something that requires real-life experience in order to truly understand and constant practice in order to master. Luckily, understanding customers and getting service experience right doesn't require a PhD. It doesn't require extensive college study, exams, or thousands of dollars in tuition, fees, and lab hours. Getting customer service started on the right track is 100 percent free. It's available to anyone who's willing to dedicate the time, effort, and attention that it requires. There are no prerequisites or no entrance exams, but it does require commitment in order to learn.

HIT THE BOOKS

Although there are plenty of businesses that have recommended reading lists for their employees, very few make reading a particular book mandatory. They might feel it's a bit too heavy-handed, but there's nothing wrong with educating your staff and expecting a particular level of customer service. You can make this a formal training event where your employees are required to have read a certain book by a specified date. When hiring new customer service agents, make certain books and courses required reading as part of their orientation.

The employees who flake out and don't follow through with your instructions are the ones who aren't taking your business as seriously as you do. So this process will also help you discern the dedicated and sincere, and weed out the ones who are simply looking to drag themselves into work and provide the least amount of effort possible to scrape by with a paycheck.

SOME RECOMMENDED READING

There are entire courses you can purchase in order to motivate and educate your workforce. However, this isn't the most cost-effective option to begin with because you might not know for sure yet who's truly serious about providing excellent customer service and who isn't. As a result, you could be spending thousands of dollars on a collective company class when some of the attendees will refuse to get anything out of it.

For simplicity's sake, we'll start with two books.

Delivering Happiness

If you know anything about Zappos, it's probably that it is famous for having legendary customer service. Tony Hsieh, the CEO of Zappos, wrote a book so that others might learn to handle customers as well as the Zappos employees do. His book is called *Delivering Happiness: A Path to Profits, Passion, and Purpose* (Business Plus 2010) and is designed to help educate both you and your employees on how to make outstanding customer service the responsibility of all people in the company, not just a single department. It will help any business understand the power of creating a harmonious environment and the incredible positive effects it will have on customers.

Raving Fans

Look on Amazon for Ken Blanchard's book, *Raving Fans: A Revolutionary Approach to Customer Service* (William Morrow 1993). You'll find tons of reviews from business owners on how the lessons and principles in Blanchard's book have either improved their business and bottom line, or turned the business around from seemingly impending collapse. If you love it, then make sure your employees get educated on it as well. Other fantastic and recommended books for service experience inspiration include:

▸ *Customer Satisfaction Is Worthless, Customer Loyalty Is Priceless* – Jeffery Gitomer (Bard Press 1998)
▸ *The Zappos Experience: 5 Principles to Inspire, Engage, and WOW* – Joseph Michelli (McGraw-Hill 2011)
▸ *Exceptional Service, Exceptional Profit: The Secrets of Building a Five-Star Customer Service Organization* – Leonardo Inghilleri and Micah Solomon (AMACOM 2010)
▸ *Be Our Guest: Perfecting the Art of Customer Service* – The Disney Institute and Theodore Kinni (Disney Editions 2011)

STAY ON TOP OF THE DIGITAL MOUNTAIN

There are a lot of insightful customer service articles, podcasts, and videos all over the Internet. You might think there's nothing new to find from these sources, but in reality, they sometimes offer wisdom about customer service that you won't find anywhere else. Discovering even one or two tips that you haven't heard before can be well worth the time you spend.

The key is to stay educated and on the cutting edge of customer service. Don't stop learning. Always continue your education in customer service, and make sure your employees are doing the same.

COMPETE ONLY AGAINST YOURSELF

The customer service bar is set pretty low in the world today. So low, in fact, that you could keep a business going with only medi-ocre customer service skills. But is that what you want? Do you want a business that merely survives, or do you want a thriving, suc-cessful business that can flourish in any economy? You can't achieve a paradigm-shift type of revolution in your industry by imitating what everyone else has done. Creating lasting change and keeping it going requires a fundamentally different approach to how you and your orga-nization work. It's no longer enough to just be slightly different from the alternative. In order to achieve transformational change, the type of change that takes your organization to a new level of service opera-tion, you're likely going to be on a journey of one. Comparing yourself with the competition will no longer be an effective measurement. The most accurate source of evaluation will be your own past performance.

Most businesses obsess about watching their competition, so much so that they begin to lose track of their own strengths, their own vision, and all the aspects that make them unique to the customers in their industry. Measuring your company against your closest compe-tition is easy, but that's not where you'll find success if you want to create lasting customer relationships and meaningful change. Trans-forming who you are and what you offer, improving productivity, time management, psychology of service, and the ability to act on customer insight and industry data are internally measured metrics. It's difficult to stack up your time management versus a competitor and use that as a measurement for success. All you can do is measure what you do and what the ultimate result is on the customer experience.

FOCUS ON YOU

Many businesses psych themselves out because of myopic focus on the wrong catalysts for change. Your drive should not be to be better than the other guy. Your drive should be to deliver an outstanding customer experience so that your clients return to your business again and again. How did your business do yesterday? What did you learn from the interactions you or your team had with your customers? This is such a simple observation, and it's right under your nose as a business owner, but many so-called business experts focus all their attention on a new and flashy marketing plan, or a new way to outshine their competitors.

Sometimes the most powerful adjustments you can make in your business are actually quite affordable and incredibly simple. Companies pay millions of dollars for studies and information, when they can dramatically increase their profits and client retention by learning from their own behavior, and striving to be better today than they were yesterday and better tomorrow than they are today. If you want to achieve transformational results, it's critical that you take responsibility for your own attitudes and behaviors. Move beyond the common interdependence between what you do and what your competitor does. Instead take control of service and impose your own strategy for what you want your customers to experience. This will enable you to achieve the next level of service experience where the business transaction really only happens between you and your customer. It's a level of customer loyalty and engagement where your competitors are no longer operating at the same level of services. A high school and a professional NFL football team are both playing the same game, but it's clear that there's no real comparison between the two in terms of execution.

"GOOD ENOUGH" TODAY ISN'T
GOOD ENOUGH TOMORROW

It's never profitable or advisable to focus strictly on the negative. Knowing what not to do is important, yes, but knowing exactly what to do is even more important. Consider that Thomas Edison attempted to construct the incandescent bulb many times. Did some of Edison's many prototypes function? Certainly. However, they were ineffective as reliable lightbulbs. Historians suggest that a number of other inventors had previously tackled the same challenge, yet Edison is credited with the invention, because his version proved to be the most effective solution. Each iteration of his lightbulb focused on improving upon earlier models. It took time, but eventually he got there.

Discover what aspects of customer service your business is excelling in. Even if you're just barely scraping by, you almost certainly have at least a few positive traits going for you. Observe them, document them, and gauge your customer's behavior toward your business when you express these traits. This is how companies establish a successful method of dealing with customers. The average customer service today leaves so many people starving for a better experience, but very few companies even bother to improve at all.

It's OK to periodically take note of what the competitors are doing and make evaluations compared with your overall plan, but to succeed and excel you *must* focus your attention on your own customer service policies and strive to surpass them every single day. Just as you never stop growing as an individual, neither should your business. Be sure what you're competing against is yesterday's performance. You are responsible for your own actions and possess the power of initiative to take action and make things happen. Proactive excellence means being a creator of circumstance. You are always in control of thoughts, words, and actions. You have the power to act and not be acted on.

Rule 8

STOP OVERTHINKING CUSTOMER SERVICE

Are you exhausted, overwhelmed, and burdened by the vast amounts of customer data constantly bombarding your in-box and your key metric reports? The speed of business today, with gigabytes and terabytes of customer data available, is enough to consume you if you don't learn to put it into context. In his book *Simplify: Ten Practices to Unclutter Your Soul* (Tyndale Momentum 2014), Bill Hybels wisely warns that when we spend our lives doing things that keep us busy but don't really matter, we sacrifice the things that do matter. It's astonishing how businesses spend so much time, money, and energy trying to understand customers. We all buy things; we're all customers. We all know that we prefer to be treated with respect and courtesy, so why has such a commonsense gesture become a mystery to us? It's as if customers are a different type of person altogether, when we ourselves are customers.

There isn't a one-size-fits-all approach to customer service. Certain businesses may have similarities, but each business is also unique. Your uniqueness is one of your strongest selling points to the customers to whom you want to appeal. This means that your approach to dealing with customers' needs to be customized to the type of customers your business attracts. Connecting with customers in a meaningful way doesn't always mean doing more, but doing better at what needs to be done. Instead of always looking to add, think instead what isn't needed, then cut back. Find a way to make things simpler and then simplify. Work on creating a balance in order to improve the workplace and the work life. You'll be amazed as you see real change in how your people think about, feel toward, and act with your customers.

DON'T DUMP ALL YOUR TIME
INTO PREPARATION

The term *in the trenches* applies here. That is to say, training is important, and so is the discipline of a customer service agent, but what matters even more than training is practical application and continuous learning from experience. Have you ever seen a member of a sales team who was unorthodox in his behavior and in his customer service approach, but who seemed to sell much more compared with all the other sales representatives? How about a quirky customer service representative who always seems to brighten up every customer's day, and somehow defuses the more angry customers by handling the tough questions with poise and kindness?

Not every customer service situation can be scripted or outlined in a manual. Your customer service agents will get into their stride with experience, and just as important, with a commitment to grow and improve their skills. Individuals can only know where they need room for improvement by first dealing with customers, and no amount of prep work can replace solid real-world experience. Instead of filling your to-do list with every possible action step and scripted response, eliminate the clutter from the closets and desk drawers of your mind and enable yourself to see the possibilities that lie in each customer interaction. The checklists, action guides, and talking points can be helpful, but they should never take precedence over the clarity of knowing what the customer wants and how best to deliver it.

LEARN FROM YOUR PAST,
BUT DON'T OBSESS OVER IT

The past should be for learning. When you fail, it's a learning opportunity for what you shouldn't be doing. When you succeed, it's a learning opportunity for what you should be doing, and even an idea of what you could be doing better than you currently are. Ask yourself, how hard is it to be nice? How difficult is it to listen to the desires of others and provide a solution in a friendly manner? Understanding the depth of human psychology may deserve a college course all its own, but being thoughtful and receptive to another human being isn't rocket science. It's simple, and it will serve as the backbone of your business!

Customers today don't expect *more* from you. They expect *better.* Stop overthinking customer service. Imagine how you would like to be treated (with courtesy and respect) and treat customers the same way. It's that simple; so spread the word and start doing what is effective at developing positive customer interactions and creating lasting customer relationships. There are many opportunities out there for you to make a difference. Open yourself and your organization to participate in the things that matter to customers. Don't overthink it and get bogged down in every possibility and piece of data that's available. Emphasize delivering personal customer service and create valuable products and services that make a difference to the life of the customer.

BABY STEPS TO SERVICE PERFECTION

Getting service right isn't done overnight. As you look to improve customer experience, make sure that you carefully study the needs and wants of your customers. Identify what really works, what actually matters, and what doesn't yield results. Then use those best practices in managing the experience to deliver the most value for your organization and the customers you serve.

As you take the initial baby steps toward achieving your vision for experience, you'll begin to see the value that comes from helping customers. The training and learning that you undergo will help you to walk a little taller and do a little better each day. The more refined you become in your ability to target and deliver the exact needs of your customers, the more you'll find that they'll naturally share their experiences with others around them. This will perpetuate the cycle of service as new prospects will look to you for the solution to their needs, problems, and concerns.

ASK YOURSELF THESE TWO CRITICAL QUESTIONS EVERY DAY

▶ We all want to know that we're on the right track, doing the right thing. Developing your service experience requires constant reaffirmation and validation that the work you do is right. The key to long-term success and exceptional experiences is making sure that you remain on the right track. Ben Franklin is often referred to as a "self-made man." He was an excellent example of constant self-improvement and introspection.

Franklin spent his whole life trying to do things better. In his autobiography, he outlined his detailed project of achieving moral perfection and personal development. You may not be setting out to reach such lofty goals, but you can still use Franklin's two key self-development questions as inspiration for you, your team, and your organization when you work to develop great customer service skills and exceptional customer experiences. Franklin's overall philosophy and approach to personal development teaches us about the foundation of great customer service by beginning and ending each day with a question.

QUESTION #1:
"WHAT GOOD SHALL I DO THIS DAY?"

Great customer service begins with the attitude that each day is an opportunity to do what is right for customers. This attitude inspires us to look for opportunities to make a difference. Each customer service situation we're involved in is an opportunity to change someone's day for the better. Starting our day with this mentality encourages us to fix the root of customers' problems, not just patch over some of the symptoms. Franklin adds great wisdom for those who sincerely want to make a difference:

- ▸ Always keep in your eye the Golden Rule, doing as you would be done unto.
- ▸ Be complaisant (agreeable/accommodating) to the meanest, as well as the greatest.
- ▸ If you affront (offend) in a small matter, it may probably hinder you from a future good customer.
- ▸ Strive to maintain a fair character in the world: That will be the best means for advancing your credit, gaining you the most flourishing trade, and enlarging your fortune.
- ▸ Condescend to no mean action, but add a luster to trade, by keeping up the dignity of your nature.

QUESTION #2:
"WHAT GOOD HAVE I DONE THIS DAY?"

At the close of each day, examine yourself to see if you remained true to your principles of great customer service and exceptional customer experiences. Did your actions prove your conviction of real service to your customers? Did you make a difference in resolving problems and not just patching symptoms? If you can, without question, know that you have made a difference, and specifically point out situations that demonstrate your customer-focused actions, you'll be well on your way to setting the standard for great customer service.

What Ben Franklin believed in, he believed in with a passion. Passionate belief, combined with creativity, problem-solving skills, common sense, and wisdom, are the foundation stones of developing exceptional customer experiences.

Rule 10

FIND A WAY TO SAY YES
EVEN WHEN THE ANSWER IS NO

One word holds the power of the future of the customer relationship. One word has the power to increase customer loyalty and set the stage for future business success. That word is *yes,* and being able to get there as quickly as possible in the customer interaction can make or break the perception of you and your organization in the mind of the customer. It's one of the simplest responses that you could give; yet it has a tremendous effect on the emotional state of the customer and the future of the relationship.

There's real power in being able to tell a customer yes. Likewise, there's something about telling one of your customers no that can severely harm your relationship with them. It goes beyond reason and dives directly into your customer's subconscious. I know you don't want to have to go through a psychology course before being able to understand what this means, so we'll break it down as simply as possible.

Getting to yes in a customer interaction is both an art and a science. Not every customer request can be answered with a resounding yes, but you can usually frame the customer's request in terms of possible solutions, thus appealing to the customer's expectations and demonstrating your willingness to deliver positive results. The true power of the word *yes* stems from the fact that customer interactions are generally difficult conversations. Customer interactions are often the result of failed processes. Something went wrong. Something broke. Something wasn't clear. Something didn't work. Something was missing. Something wasn't delivered.

Given the nature of customer service today, most customers approach the service interaction as a showdown at high noon. Customer service conversations too often begin as defensive battles with each side entrenched in why they're right and the other side wrong, and they generally go downhill from there. Customers and customer service agents typically listen not for meaning but for the exact words spoken. Both parties are missile-seeking targets; any misspoken word inflicts the maximum amount of damage possible, given the sensitivity of the situation.

IN THE FACE OF PROBLEMS

Having to tell customers no is typically only something that comes up in the face of a problem. They have an issue or concern that they want your business to resolve, and it's just not reasonable for you to have to do it. Sometimes it's a customer trying to return a broken product that she's had for two years, and the warranty expired after 90 days—or a customer wanting you to replace his transmission for free, simply because he's been a longtime customer for oil changes. The experience, whether during the purchase process or usage period, is critical in determining the future actions of your customer.

An American Express survey showed that 78 percent of respondents canceled a purchase or did not make a purchase simply because of a negative customer service experience.[1] Have you ever felt jilted by a business you've been loyal to for years? Has a service provider ever fallen short of what it claimed to provide? Feeling helpless, customers often feel they have no option but to go to a competitor the next time around. Bad service experience or failure to deliver with a product or service leaves a bitter taste in our mouths. It doesn't take much more than one bad experience before customers spit out the sour fruit and look for a new provider. These customer losses can—in many cases—be avoided with a little bit of flexibility, creativity, and better communication with customers.

IN A WORLD OF BLACK AND WHITE,
THINK GRAY

Yes and no aren't the only options you have. There are many circumstances where it would be easy to please a customer, but your customer service agents have become too rigid in their approach to dealing with your customers. Consider a customer who ordered something from your business but didn't realize that shipping was only free if the order was over $50. How do you handle this?

A rigid approach would be to stick with company policies:

> *"No, we've sent you what you've ordered, and we're sorry, but it's not our responsibility to compensate you for the shipping charges on this order."*

Do you think that customer will ever grace you with her business again? What if, instead, you took a more appealing approach? Note that the first option says yes to free shipping on this order but draws a line there (no repeat misunderstandings), while the second approach preserves the principle of charging for shipping under $50, but offers an incentive for the customer to come back with a free month of premium service.

Option 1

"We're really sorry for the misunderstanding. You see, it's our company policy that our clients pay for the cost of shipping under $50, but we understand that you were unaware of this when you placed your order. Because of this, we would be more than willing to compensate you for the shipping costs for this order. We strive to make your customer experience fantastic and hope you will visit us again soon!"

Option 2

"We are really sorry for the misunderstanding. Although our company policy is to offer free shipping for orders of $50 or more, we really appreciate your business, and as a goodwill gesture, we would

like to give you a $20 credit for your next order. We strive to make your customer experience a fantastic one, and really hope that you'll visit us again in the near future!"

Be creative, be flexible, and be accommodating—but for the sake of your business, do everything you can to avoid saying no. Instead of picking sides, realize that in order to achieve long-term success, there's really only one side you can ever choose: the side of the customer. When faced with a difficult interaction, quickly establish your loyalties on behalf of serving the customer. Use this initial opportunity to validate the customer's concern and enlist the customer on your mission to uncover the cause of the problem. Instead of agent versus customer, the battle then is agent and customer versus the problem. Once this is done, difficult conversations then can continue without defensiveness. Speaking and listening will be focused on meaning and not technicality. Customers and those who serve them will remain impartial and balanced through the process of identifying problems in processes and working through the solutions to solve the deficiency in service.

Decide to emphasize the positive and see the possibilities in what you have available to you. Learn to address the most common customer requests using the power of positive language, even when the answer to that request might technically be no. The greatest obstacle in each interaction and the key to ensuring that you get another chance to keep your customer is being able to satisfy the needs of customers. As you understand your role in facilitating each interaction and learning to fine-tune your available resources, you'll begin to lay the groundwork for understanding and influencing customer relationships in a positive way.

Rule 11

LOVE YOUR CRITICS

Don't you just *love* angry customers? Seriously. Don't you? OK, maybe in the heat of the moment, it's difficult to appreciate an unreasonable or angry customer, and that's understandable. However, after you calm down and the tension of the moment has passed, your most critical customers are those who most often give you the opportunity to learn a valuable lesson about your service delivery. The situations that are most tense are often the situations from which you can learn from the most. Don't ever disregard a critical customer and let your opportunity for growth slip through your fingers. Opportunities for learning from our past performances are all around you, and you should embrace feedback that exposes potential flaws in your service strategy.

Your first overly critical customer review will hurt. Really bad. There's no way around it. It's bound to happen, and you need to simply move on. My team's first-ever scathing review hurt. The customer clearly overreacted, but that's beside the point. When you're known as kings of customer service, even a so-so customer experience can seem to customers like the sky is falling down.

THE MEANING BEHIND THE WORDS

When it comes to customer service, communication is key. Do you *really* understand what the customer is saying? If not, how can you find out as quickly as possible? If you aren't sure of what the customer meant or if the customer responds that your answer wasn't what he was looking for, you have a choice to make. Do you keep playing customer service ping pong, going back and forth answering the customer's questions, or do you change the game altogether by getting at the core of what the customer really wants you to do?

Part of the process of growing and learning is failing. Critics are your most reliable source of truth when it comes to those failures and the opportunities for growth and development that come from failing. There's no denying that it's challenging to receive criticism, but within the criticism you're offered a chance to review the established framework you've developed. You can closely scrutinize and determine if the various components truly are contributing to the overall vision you want to achieve. Criticism sheds light in areas of service and action that you might not otherwise consider during the normal course of business.

CONTRAST AND STRATEGY

Have you noticed that once you go through a hardship, another similar hardship just doesn't seem as bad as the first one? That's because the shock of something new and difficult is harsh, but once it's over and you learn from it, you grow and adapt so that next time it takes less of a toll and you're better prepared to handle it. This is known as *contrast*, and times of contrast are pure gold for learning how to better handle your most critical customers.

What about strategy? Just being able to smile and keep a good attitude when dealing with a critical customer is definitely good, but you don't just want to become a more resilient punching bag. How can you use these contrasting opportunities to adjust your approach to customer service? Build a strategy based on feedback.

Even if a customer is unreasonable, think about what exactly is the real reason for the complaint. Perhaps he was mistreated the last time he visited your business, and now he's demanding ridiculous levels of compensation in order to remain a customer. What's there to learn in this? An opportunity presents itself to analyze how your staff conducts business with your customers. You might learn of a slacking employee, or you might learn about insecurities or problems that a customer has that your business can fix with just a few adjustments.

The DigiCert customer support team is known for its outstanding technical support for server and network administrators securing their websites with SSL Certificates. The DigiCert team leads its industry in service rating and has the most five-star reviews of any other SSL provider in the industry. While the thousands of positive experiences and five-star reviews are validation that the company's framework for service works for its customers, it's the lone two-star review the team received once that stands out as one of the most important lessons learned. A nontechnical customer struggled through a specific process inside the customer account and, while frustrated, posted a review complaining that the process was overly complicated for a nontechnical person. Although easy to dismiss as an outlier, the two-star review serves as an important reminder that not all customers are the same. Careful attention must be paid to ensure that new products, services, or account changes are evaluated for usability and simplicity to ensure exceptional service for all customers.

EMBRACE THE CRITIC

The power of social networks has increased the impact of customer reviews today. In today's digital age, what your customers think and feel are processed at the speed of light and instantly distributed throughout the world for almost anyone to see. Controversy is always popular, and a negative experience can take on a life of its own. Success today isn't achieved by just acquiring more customers than your competitors; you have to ensure that you consistently stay on top of customer needs and take care of any customer concerns that arise. The combined impact of smartphones and mobile technology, along with the rise of social media and social networking, has created new business transparencies. As a result, organizations today must relearn how to work with customers.

DON'T IGNORE NEGATIVITY

Staying relevant today means knowing exactly what your customers are saying and knowing how to best respond to what's being said.

Any negativity could be the beginning of bigger problems with your customers. Engaging with customers on good and bad service reviews is an opportunity that organizations today shouldn't ignore.

Customer feedback offers the chance to have a constructive dialogue with customers and other community members who see the results of your service. Oftentimes, critical feedback arises from customers who simply are looking for sincerity, attention, and restitution for something that happened beyond their control. A quick response or thoughtful action can often defuse even the harshest critics today.

TIMELY RESPONSES ARE CRITICAL

Everyone knows how fast an angry rant can be posted, seen, liked, and shared; they also know that once it's out there, it's there. If you're faced with a negative review, the best move is to immediately open the doors of communication and apologize, whether via social network, email, or personal phone call. Then do something to make it right: Offering a refund, store credit, or a coupon is usually well received. Doing something special, outside of the normal business interaction, shows you care about providing the very best customer service experience and does wonders to create and maintain a positive reputation with customers.

Whether it's to feature a new service, include a new product, or even to redesign the way your business approaches customer interaction—be grateful for your most critical customers. It's no fun dealing with them at the time, certainly, but they are often the biggest factors when it comes to making positive changes in your own business that will affect every customer down the line. Once you look at everything your most critical customers have helped you establish, you'll welcome the rest in with open arms.

CREATE YOUR DOS AND DON'TS OF SERVICE

One important fact to consider (before reading any further about exceptional customer service) is that customer support and care for customer relationships has typically been done very poorly in recent years. This is evident by the number of negative reputations and viral stories of terrible customer service and customer experiences gone wrong. Bad reputations for service have only promoted additional mistrust among customers; it seems like few customers truly trust the organizations that serve them. Most customer relationships today are left to deteriorate after the initial customer sale. Even with examples of a few major brands breaking the mold, considerable time and effort are needed to put this big bad customer support picture right again overall.

To make sure you're on the right track, you need to establish your own set of rules for how to deliver high-quality customer service. There are dos and don'ts in how to behave with customers, and it's essential that you communicate those clearly and effectively to everyone who can affect the ultimate service result.

Here are a few dos and don'ts to get you started in developing your own list based on the specific needs of your organization and the wants of your customers.

DO ENCOURAGE INITIATIVE

Initiative often leads to memorable experiences. Employees who are encouraged to think on their own will often come up with innovative ideas and unique approaches to resolve everyday customer problems. Each customer problem should be seen as an opportunity for self-motivated employees to deliver outstanding customer service. Freedom to act innovatively in service interactions will foster teamwork and develop a fun and positive environment for service teams.

DO THINK POSITIVE

Optimistic and positive thinking (particularly when interacting with customers today) is the key to a great customer satisfaction experience, and it also boosts confidence and raises employee morale. Being real and keeping things in perspective also play an important role, along with the positivism and optimism.

You are unique. Developing your own style means your behaviors and actions reflect your personality and your individuality. When you are true to yourself, your positive attitude will shine through to customers. Interacting with the customers in a personal, purposeful, and helpful manner is a highly effective way to develop meaningful customer relationships and memorable service experiences.

DO ENCOURAGE CLOSE ENGAGEMENT

In a customer support scenario, the customer needs to be told all the things that can be done, what will be done, and when it will be done. Real service is about solving problems and offering solutions, giving the customer relief from any further burdening effects of the problem in a warm, engaging, and polite way.

Customers today desperately need a friendly human being who is real and able to engage with them instinctively. They crave emotional connection. The company relies on its employees to deliver an exceptionally memorable and positive experience. It is those pleasant experiences that actually encourage everlasting customer loyalty. Great, reliable service breeds a good reputation, which is also flattered by the free, positive promotion via independent reviews, reports, or verbal recommendation.

DON'T MAKE IT PERSONAL

Employees should not bring their own personal problems into the workplace. They should be determined, focused, and effective at dealing with any customer problems when they arise and not let outside problems cloud their judgment, throw them off track, or cause them to send mixed messages. Employees should not get frustrated with a customer's demands no matter how unreasonable they may seem to be. They should keep the discussion going in a friendly, fact-finding manner, listening closely to what the customer is really saying. And they should definitely not lose patience if they find themselves explaining something to a customer over and over. The reason something has to be explained again may very well be that the employee did not explain it effectively the first time. All of us as individuals learn things in different ways.

DON'T PROJECT A COLD ATTITUDE

Employees should not spoil an opportunity to develop relationships with the customers by acting or talking like obedient corporate robots. Stiff, unemotional, by-the-books discourse will never create the warm give-and-take atmosphere needed to deal with a customer's problems. Personality, conversation, and talking about the issue at hand (as a central theme of focus) are all important in establishing relationships. Building a two-way rapport with customers is not going to happen effectively without projecting personality, especially if the conversation lacks stimulation and is not focused on anything of mutual interest or relevant.

You must have certain rules and regulations to help the smooth running of any business or institution. However, simply preaching corporate policy doesn't always lead to solutions for customers. The potential for effective customer relationship building can't happen if the opportunity is constantly squandered by cold, unfriendly corporate policies. If there were one place where solutions are most critical to continued success, it would be in customer service interactions. Serving customers and meeting their needs are key to continued business success.

EXPLOIT YOUR CUSTOMER'S PAIN POINTS, BUT NEVER EXPLOIT YOUR CUSTOMERS

A customer's pain point is a clear opportunity for action. Exploiting your customers' pain points is about giving them what *they* want, not selling them what *you* want them to buy. This really is as easy as it sounds, but so many businesses never seem to catch on. The trick is that nobody likes to be "sold." *"Here's why you need our fantastic new product! Your life is dull and bland without our magical trinket, so buy it now, you'll be glad you did!"* Sound cheesy? It is, but it's also the basic essence of what most customers hear when listening to the average salesperson. Sometimes they'll buy into what you're selling, but that's the thing; they shouldn't need to be convinced to buy something!

The real power in exploiting your customers' pain points is giving them what they already want. How is that so hard? If a man came crawling out of the desert, asking for a glass of water, would you try to pitch him on how awesome your new energy drink product is? On how it can revitalize him and replenish his electrolytes? I hope your answer is, "Of course not!"

Far too many companies are trying to sell people on what the company wants to sell. Consider the concept of cold-calling—employees aren't calling people who want what you offer; they're just spamming telephones, asking people to buy what you want them to buy. Cold callers try to convince people how great their company's product is; they do *not* attempt to deliver what the customer truly desires.

DO WHAT THE COMPETITION IS TOO BLIND TO DO

I don't encourage you to be obsessed with what your competitors are doing, but having a decent understanding of what's going on around you is always a good idea for your business. If you observe your competitors, you'll probably find that they're trying to sell their customers on something. They're asking customers to choose their product or service, listing all their credentials, and citing all the sources that add to their credibility.

Average customers don't care about any of this stuff! All they want is the answer to this question: "I have a problem that I need solved, can you help me?" That's it! Here's how the conversation with the man who just came crawling out of the desert should go:

MAN: "Please, can you give me a glass of water? I'm very thirsty."
YOU: "Yes, sir, that will be $2.50."
MAN: "Here's $3; keep the change."
YOU: "Here's your water; enjoy!"

End of transaction.

Someone wanted something and you delivered. Position yourself this way in everything you do. Don't "sell" your customers; find out what they want, their pain points, the points that they are so obviously displaying, their clear desire that needs to be fulfilled—and then fulfill it. They want water? Give them water. If you don't have water, shape your business so that you do have water the next time they come around. All you have to do is give your customers what they ask for and they will flock to your business, returning time and time again.

UNDERSTANDING YOUR CUSTOMERS

Think of your customers as they go about their day. What frustrates them? What do they struggle with each day? What problem can you solve that would make the difference between a good and bad day for your customer? Being the difference to your customers means understanding your customers, the way they do things, and the problems they have. How do they see themselves? How do they see what they do? What motivates them? What do they really need? The opportunities exist for you to make that difference and exploit the pain points your customers endure each day.

Learning about customer pain points will help you to truly understand the customer. In-depth studies or interviews with customers can help uncover typical frustrations that customers encounter each day. Sales and customer service people can provide frontline reports. Demand more feedback from your people and enable customers to provide feedback during every touch point and in every customer interaction. Formal market research can give you great insight into entire segments of customers or industry conditions and future trends. But truly connecting with the individual customer has to be done on a one-on-one basis. Only at this level are you able to get into the mind of the customer.

TARGETING PAIN POINTS

Pain, fear, and frustration are real motivators. As human beings, we're hardwired to want to avoid pain and discomfort. We fear pain and will go to great lengths to make sure that it doesn't happen to us. Once it does, we learn our lessons and will put extreme rules and cautions all around us to avoid future pain and suffering.

If you control the information or the ability for a customer to avoid pain, you have an advantage. Solve existing pains your customer suffers and you'll find value for your organization today. Go even further to remain relevant by exploring, understanding, and innovating to solve any future possible pains that your customer may encounter and you will remain relevant for life. Ask yourself these critical questions:

1. What is the real source of the customer pain?
2. Who will benefit the most from solving this pain point?
3. Who will ultimately decide and/or pay for the solution to the pain?

4. Is there a significant enough group of customers willing to pay for a solution to the pain?
5. Are alternatives to my solution difficult to obtain in order for customers to desire to continue using my solution for their pain?

Targeting and solving customer pain points is one of the most effective strategies you can use to differentiate yourself from the hundreds of other possible solutions your customers are pitched on a daily basis. Once you break out of the initial role of just another company marketing something and step into the role of trusted problem solver, your customer relationships reach a completely different level. You are no longer a seller but a solution provider. As you develop your role of solution provider, you'll begin to see customers turn to you first for additional solutions and enhancements to existing products and services instead of to unproven competitors.

A word of caution: Never use a customer pain point as a strategic advantage over the customer. Pain points are business opportunities, not opportunities to exploit. There's a fine line between running a profitable business by addressing real problems and exploiting problems to extort additional profit. Exploiting pain is the way to the dark side of customer service. Imagine this scenario:

MAN: "Please, can you give me a glass of water? I'm very thirsty."
YOU: "You don't really want water; you want our awesome new energy drink. It's only $10."
MAN: "I just want water, and I only have $5!"
YOU: "Oh, all right. Water is $5 today—or you could put $5 down on our Energy Drink of the Month Club."
MAN: "Here's five bucks. Just give me the water."

End of transaction.
      Taking advantage of customers builds resentment and develops a new source of frustration, which will turn away customers and completely erode the customer relationship. Scorned and frustrated cus-

tomers have turned to alternative solution providers and even gone so far as helping a competitor build a similar product or service just to spite a bad service provider. And scorned customers will go to unimaginable lengths to tell the world about their terrible experience.

CUSTOMERS EXPECT AND DREAD
THE ONSLAUGHT OF ADVERTISEMENTS

Things have changed in terms of marketing these days and it has nothing to do with the products being marketed. What's changed are the people being marketed to. For many reasons, people are more skeptical, less receptive, and more discerning than ever, especially on the frontier of marketing, the Internet. But why has this happened? And how much blame can be assigned to companies?

There was a time when creating a blog, loading it up with keywords, and putting up Google AdSense text ads was an almost guaranteed moneymaking formula. Those days are gone, no matter what web entrepreneurs might tell you. Web users quickly learned to distinguish what was an honest link and what was an ad. Furthermore, pay-per-click ads became more aggressive. Popup ads and embedded video ads became something that web users not only didn't click on, but something they held in genuine contempt.

Honest and service-oriented marketers suffered for this shift. Aggressive advertisements created a digital era where users were skeptical to the point that they rejected anything that felt like an advertisement. Even companies that attempt to run honest online marketing campaigns feel the cynicism. *Trolling,* or mocking a company's Twitter or Facebook account, is often seen as funny; it's viewed as giving companies "what they deserve."

DON'T MARKET; MAKE A DIFFERENCE

Don't market your product online. Market the lifestyle that your product will help to create. Once you have created an effective community and audience via your digital marketing efforts, push the lifestyle that represents your brand. This is trickier than merely bombarding your audience with pitches for your product or company, but it is incredibly effective. In this skeptical age, it's not enough to just throw up a bunch of links and hope something sticks. Instead, you have to be savvy. But if you play the online marketing game right, the results will be well worth it.

DON'T BE ZAPPOS TO YOUR JACK WELCH CUSTOMERS

When you consider that it costs much more to acquire a new customer than it does to simply keep an existing customer, you can't afford to mess around when it comes to customer service. It's critical that you completely understand your customer and what your customer really wants from you. Simply satisfactory customer service will not cut it if you hope to raise your level of standards in the competitive customer service business arena.

The trick is that customers come in all shapes and sizes. Not all customers are looking for wacky customer service antics. More often than not, customer service is about being quick, professional, and extremely effective at delivering solutions. A Zappos style of a little bit weird is fun, but it can prove disastrous when you're dealing with Jack Welch–type customers.

TAILOR YOUR APPROACH TO THE CUSTOMER

Jack Welch is a battle-hardened, successful businessman who was the chairman and CEO of General Electric from 1981 to 2001. His net worth is over $750 million, and he's the coauthor of the bestselling business books *Winning* (HarperBusiness 2005) and *Jack: Straight from the Gut* (Business Plus 2001). Why does this matter? Because you don't want to bring a quirky and playful attitude to a customer who only wants the facts, who puts a lot of value on his time, or who depends on you for service that could have dramatic effects on their organization or bottom line. Delivering a phenomenal customer experience isn't always one-size-fits-all. The Jack Welch customers of the world want to get in, get down to business, and be done. They have laser-like focus and the way for you to cater to these customers is to really get to know what they need. Fun and quirky service is great for most people, but when you're dealing with a Jack Welch type, change your approach to an all-business mindset.

Most of the customers who walk through your door are normal people, starved for attention and a good customer service experience. This is part of why Zappos thrives so greatly in the customer service world. Many people believe that Zappos's methods are "out there," but they only seem that way now because so few companies are incorporating such successful methods into their business. Think of it like in a movie. You see a wealthy person check into a hotel or get his car from a chauffeur, and the customer service agents handle things instantly, with, "Good evening, Mr. Welch. Here's the key to your room; please enjoy your stay with us." Or, "Here's your vehicle, Mr. Welch. We greatly appreciate your visit." What's the key element here? Time! Notice how the friendly customer service element is still intact. There's no blandness or passive behavior. It's very active and swift. The respect and courtesy is present, with a high focus on time. This is how you need to handle your Jack Welch–type customers.

As a business, you may prefer more easygoing and open customers, Zappos-type customers. This doesn't mean that the more "down to business" style customers should be turned away or avoided. They're not bad customers by any means, they're just a bit different in personality. Their money is as green as any other, and when you can easily cater to both the Zappos and the Jack Welches of the world, your flexibility in being diverse will net you loads of customers of all types. And as I'm sure you're well aware, more customers means a bigger bottom line.

KNOW WHAT'S RIGHT FOR YOUR CUSTOMERS

Ultimately, it's not about what's right, but about being right for your customer. Your service experience will be more effective if you can clearly define who you are, what you do, and how you serve your customers. Your organization and its people must be clear as to who your customers really are, and they must understand how those customers need to be served. Zappos customers expect a little bit of weird and over-the-top friendly and personal interaction. For IBM customers, a more professional, defined, and structured process may be best suited in order to obtain consistent interactions and results. Neither approach is necessarily right or wrong, but each is best suited for the specific needs and expectations of the customers served.

Some organizations will face the decision to sacrifice some things in order to take care of the needs of their core customers. Zappos probably won't win major enterprise merchandise contracts, and it is fine with that. IBM won't do as well with the individual consumer market. Once you've accepted your core customers, you can plan better, allocate resources more effectively, and track the development of the customer experience in greater detail. You improve not only your ability to serve but also the effectiveness of your service.

Rule 15

MAKE YOUR CUSTOMER SERVICE A HUMAN INTERACTION

Once upon a time, we were able to go down to the market and tell the grocer what we'd like, and then the grocer would fetch it for us. We discovered that allowing people to shop for themselves and then check out was more time efficient, because everybody could get what they needed at once, rather than having to be assisted one at a time. Historically, customer service has been mainly delivered in person or over the phone. Although new channels have enabled customer interactions to take place in new and innovative ways, the level of human interaction and satisfaction continues to be highest with contact channels that rely on a more hands-on approach.

Ultimately, for the sake of cutting costs and reducing time (though mostly cutting costs), we've all but alienated customers through automation and various other methods of detachment. They're treated as little more than drones to suck money out of, and many of them feel that way. Yet because of the importance of service, the profit from customer retention, and the lifetime value of customers, the contact center continues to be a key operation for businesses today. The contact center is still the most common way customers interact with businesses. With the development of social media contact channels, this emphasis on the contact center has only enhanced the ability for service agents to deliver more personal service. Even self-service technology solutions still require humans behind the scenes to develop content, offer solutions, update, and curate the specific key details that customers rely on for service.

THE HUMAN TOUCH

While much of the attention from executives today has been on technology to eliminate the need for human service interactions, when people are fed through a mechanical process as if their every need will be taken care of by a categorizer, they feel like faceless, nameless numbers. Treating customers like a number is a dangerous trap. No one actually sets out to do it, but the more customers you acquire, the easier it becomes to be disconnected from the actual customers served.

When service decision makers become detached from the customers serviced, customers become objects to handle or issues to resolve, rather than individuals with issues to respectfully address. Does this mean you should eliminate all your automating processes? Or should you throw away all reports, dashboards, and metrics? Of course not. Mechanical features like websites, auto-responders, and newsletters serve their purpose, definitely, but they can still be given a human touch. Organizations leading the service revolution have learned to master handling simple transactions using sophisticated systems and processes that include self-service portals and automated systems in conjunction with traditional interpersonal human channels in order to complement the service experience.

Imagine how a potential prospect or customer would feel to receive a generic noreply@ email from your business. Every day, you spend countless hours and valuable resources trying to convince customers that you actually care. But do you really? You care so much about how your customers feel that you told them not to respond to you?

People aren't as stupid as many marketing firms make them out to be. After all, they're inundated with other people's marketing every day. They catch on to the tricks fast. There's only one way to truly keep customers captivated and coming back to your business. You need to make them happy, and you do that by forming a strong, lasting relationship. No amount of clever marketing or slick sales jargon can substitute for a real human connection with a customer.

INTERCONNECTING

Imagine that a customer is browsing your website, and then she's greeted with a small chat popup. On the other end of this popup is one of your customer service agents. The customer decides to use the chat popup, asking questions of the customer service agent until her concerns and questions are adequately addressed.

Now imagine that customer comes into your business in person, and she meets face-to-face with the customer service agent who helped her online. What a powerful way to use technology to not only give customer service a human touch but to enhance it! A customer is not a number, and neither are your agents. If customers must go through an automated service, such as a phone call or an online ticket, then never, ever refer to your customers, or the agents helping them, as numbers. If "Jared Martins" is the customer's name, then that should be what your agent sees. If your agent is "Jamie Elvidge from Platteville, Wisconsin," then the customer should see or hear Jamie on the other end. If your agent is Luis Merino from Henderson, Nevada, then the customer should experience an interaction with Luis, not with a generic robot spitting out the customer service one-liners. People connect with people, not systems.

The best customer service isn't done by systems, but by real people who understand how to get the most *from* systems in order to deliver the exact type of service experience customers need. When customers have problems, they want a real person to help them. Don't use technology as a substitute for human interaction. Give your customers that human touch and let technology help with that effort.

Rule 16

MICROMANAGE EVERY DAY

▶ Every employee loves a micromanaging boss—someone to tell them what to do, how to do it, and constantly breathe down their necks when it isn't done just perfectly. Wait a minute . . . that's the kind of micromanaging that *nobody* likes, right? We've grown to see micromanaging as a bad thing because of how it's been abused. All sarcasm aside, it's no fun when a supervisor, manager, or boss is constantly scrutinizing your every action. So what's good about micromanaging? As it turns out, when you lack complete knowledge of a system, a product, or service, micromanaging is the right way to carry you through the process of learning, while still delivering the service results that customers want.

Good micromanaging is better described as *close managing*. It can be an excellent source of constant feedback in situations where team members are still learning to adapt to their roles or when the organization is facing a new challenge for which it lacks the established systems and protocols. When high-value, critical projects exist, it's imperative that leaders make themselves readily available and guide the team through the specific requirements of the project. When projects that cannot be allowed to fail crop up, leaders must step in and ensure that every component within the organization works flawlessly. This means being more involved and hands-on throughout the development of the project.

Find every component within your sphere of influence and do whatever it takes to see that it works or change it. Some underperforming processes can be delegated; others will require more time and attention directly from you. Naturally, the need for micromanaging will diminish as people and processes become more refined and start working as intended to deliver the results that customers want. But as new people are hired and more complex challenges arise, you'll be required to dedicate additional time, insight, and hands-on work until people and processes can perform at the highest level on their own. Make it perfectly clear to team members why you're getting involved and what your role will be throughout the process. Never use micromanaging as a standard way of doing business. Train your people and develop frameworks for operation in a way that the need for micromanaging diminishes each day.

GOOD MICROMANAGING

The good kind of micromanaging is not micromanaging the things your employees do, but instead micromanaging *why* they do these things. Think of it as being super detail-oriented, but in a way that doesn't anger or annoy your workforce. This isn't about constantly trying to shape employees a certain way, but about building a framework for your business and constantly improving on it. The employees will need training and appropriate workplace conditioning, certainly, but what good is micromanaging an employee to be the perfect customer service agent for an imperfect work system? Ask yourself:

▸ Why do I have my customer service agents do what they do?
▸ Is there a way to make contacting clients easier for my staff?
▸ Do the rules and policies my company has in place provide an outstanding customer experience, or do some of them hurt the customer experience?
▸ Is my business set up to handle customer email and messages in the most professional and efficient manner possible?
▸ Several customers have expressed the wish that we provide our services more quickly for them. How can I improve the process without paying too much or sacrificing the quality of the customer service experience?

These questions may seem a bit broad, but contemplating them in a wider spectrum allows you to narrow the ways you can improve the way your company does business, which, in turn, improves your customer service. This process of getting down to the more intricate parts of your business framework and changing what needs to be changed on the microscopic level is the kind of micromanaging you should be doing on a daily basis!

When performance has been substandard and team members require additional coaching and development, leaders and managers need to take a more proactive role in ensuring that the deliverables to the organization go through the proper review process and are filtered to ensure that they meet the needs of the organization and senior leaders. Feedback and review before delivering is critical under these circumstances.

THINK 80/80, NOT 80/20

The Pareto principle, most commonly known as the 80/20 rule, states that 20 percent of your business is responsible for 80 percent of your profits.[1] The 80/20 rule is part of Business 101 today; the problem is that it's often misinterpreted. The Pareto principle dates back to 1896 and is thought to have been developed based on Vincent Pareto's observations of Italian landownership or from his observation that 20 percent of pea pods in his garden accounted for 80 percent of all peas grown.[2] While this may still hold true for some circumstances, the way we do business today can be vastly different from Italian landownership at the turn of the 20th century, and most of us aren't in the gardening business. If you step back and look at the realities of business and revenue generated, while your emphasis may still be on the 20 percent you consider your top customers, oftentimes they don't account for 80 percent of the total revenue for your business. The power of technology and the information available to customers today are pushing us toward an age where 80 percent of customers could really account for 80 percent of the revenue of the business, an 80/80 split. In other cases, you might actually see 20 percent of customers generating an even greater percentage than 80 percent of the revenue to the business.[3] The challenge, however, is that while one customer might not contribute direct profit because of a small transaction value, it is more difficult to determine how much that customer's experience might generate or undermine future business because of the customer's subsequent promotion of or negative comments about the company. A nonprofitable customer might be vocal enough to affect subsequent revenue from other customers in a positive or negative way.

In short, every customer matters today. Customers are empowered and comfortable researching alternatives; social media and technology have given tremendous power to customers to voice their opinions of the good and bad they see in products or services provided. Staying relevant today and engaging with customers in a way that matters and keeps their loyalty requires a shift in how we approach customer value. Some companies have policies that were established 15 or 20 years ago, and are still being used to this day. Have those policies been reevaluated to reflect the new requirements of today's customers? Have policies been reconfirmed that they still apply to today's business conditions? Many policies exist not because they are necessarily the best for the customers but simply because the business has gotten so used to adhering to specific policy that it doesn't even think about changing it. Every organization should have processes and systems in place to continually reevaluate its policies, processes, and actions against the needs and wants of its customers, as well as current business conditions.

Get down to the deepest details. Throw out the junk, replace what doesn't work, design new policies, incorporate new training, set new standards, and so on. Design a framework that's perfect for your business and *then* have your employees change to match it, rather than forcing them to adhere to outdated and inefficient policies and principles.

It's time for you to start micromanaging.

DO CUSTOMER SERVICE ON DAY ONE OF THE JOB

Learning in real life is about on-the-job training. When it's your turn, it's time to perform. Human beings are *designed* to learn from experiences. In a job setting, you observe what you're taught by the veterans and then mimic them so you can get the same successful results. If you're still sending your customer service representatives through a typical four- to six-week training course in order to get them up to speed with how business is done, consider restructuring how your new employee training takes place.

OVERCOMING THE FEAR OF NEW

One of the most frustrating experiences as an employee is starting a new job. Most of us leave a job for a better opportunity. But no matter what our level of expertise, when we start a new job we all get thrown back into the beginner level at the new organization. We all have to cope with new systems, new workflows, and new people to work with. For an experienced veteran, it can be a maddening experience to leave a job where one is operating at a master level and become an apprentice again in a new location.

Years ago, I suffered through this when I left a system administrator engineer position to join a newly organized startup in my industry. It was an opportunity that I couldn't pass up. At my previous job, I was at the top of my industry. I trained the top-tier agents and took on the issues that the escalation agents couldn't handle. But in my new position, even though I understood the nature of the work and the answers to the questions customers had, learning a new system and understanding the proper workflow for how solutions should be implemented took quite a long time. Comparing my level of productivity on the new job with the old one was demoralizing.

LEARNING IN REAL TIME

If trainings are done in short modules, followed up by monitored real live work, then instead of taking weeks to learn new systems, new employees can begin to taste success in their new roles on day one. Rather than waiting weeks to actually do real work, they have the opportunity to contribute in their new role from the very first day. The cases they work on might be simple, and the new employees might not participate in every customer contact channel, but hours after starting a new job, employees can begin to feel the satisfaction that comes from actually contributing to the work they were hired to do.

Orientation and HR paperwork can all be done before the first day of work, and if not, it can always be done later on the first day. But connecting real, productive, effective work with a new employee on the first day is a boost to the morale of customer service agents. This boost is critical because new agents will always take some time before they become 100 percent effective in their role. Being able to see productive work getting done will carry them through the time it'll take before they fully understand the systems and workflows of work.

Consider the traditional approach of training and then doing. Let's say a new team member, having been trained, now speaks with a customer and definitely seems to be handling things all right, but then the customer has a fairly simple question that the new agent can't seem to answer. Now the agent has to go speak with a more experienced representative to get the answer to help the customer, thus costing the customer and other employees time. Both employees and customers will expect a "trained" representative to perform better than a standard fresh hireling. But consider this: four to six weeks in a training environment may give a new customer service agent an idea of how to do their job, but it's not the same as gaining actual experience. You can read a book about climbing Mount Everest, but it's nothing like actually climbing Everest.

WORKING IN THE TRENCHES

Being educated on how to work a job is a good thing; I'm not saying that it's bad. There is a difference, though, in being educated and being dragged through a process that simply isn't a worthwhile substitute for real experience. So what can you do instead? Simple: Put them into the field with an experienced customer service representative. Let them learn while gaining experience. On-the-job training is a fantastic way to build them up into highly capable employees. Consider the following benefits of on-the-job training for your customer service agents:

- ▸ You save expenses on sending them to a four- to six-week course.
- ▸ You give them a taste of real work so they know what to expect.
- ▸ They get trained by a veteran employee, not some one-size-fits-all training outfit.
- ▸ They can be conditioned a little more each day, rather than being thrown into the job after they've been officially "trained."

They can start small, learning to answer customer service emails, learning how to appropriately respond to the customer's concerns and questions. After the new hireling becomes more familiar and comfortable with those tasks, she can be moved to working with customers personally, perhaps taking calls or tending to customers in person. It's all about integrating them steadily into the workplace responsibilities until they're ready to do things on their own. Getting a good start with customer service is critical for organizations that emphasize the service experience.

Connecting every employee, regardless of the position, with the service process helps keep the entire organization aware of the service focus. Zappos, for example, requires every new employee to spend the first two weeks on the job working the front lines of customer service. Everyone has to answer phones, handle emails, and really learn to connect with customers. Following their customer service experience, new employees also spend a full week in the Zappos warehouse in Kentucky doing order fulfillment so they truly understand and connect with the products their customers want. Getting everyone directly connected with what you *really* do for customers is critical in order to unite a team and deliver exceptional results.

BE THE WORST ON YOUR TEAM

▶ It might sound strange to say you should be the worst on your team, but consider this for a moment: Who should you hire? Do you hire people to replace you at what you do? Rarely. Typically, you hire people to fill the positions that you either can't do or don't want to do. If you're not exceptional at customer service, then you hire people who are. If you're not that good at setting up business infrastructure, then you hire somebody who is. What about information technology? Do you know how to operate and maintain servers for your business? Most people don't, so you hire someone who can.

OVERCOMING THE BOZO EXPLOSION

Guy Kawasaki, one of Apple's first employees and evangelist of the Macintosh computer, refers the slippery slope of hiring as *the bozo explosion*. Normally, A-class players in an organization recruit and hire other A-class players. However, B-class players generally operate under a difference assumption about talent and their own place within the team. B-class players often have the negative tendency to see other talent and skill as threats to their position. They tend to hire C-class players in order to compensate for their own fears and weaknesses.

The problem becomes more prominent with lower-grade team members who consistently hire beneath them and create an underperforming team simply to maintain their own superiority. This situation perpetuates itself, and eventually you're left with an organization of D-class players. This sets up a dangerous path to failure and layoffs all around.

In reality, A-class level players realize that their value isn't derived from their superiority compared with the people underneath them, but rather in their ability to attract the best talent and create a team of high performers for the organization. A-class players have the tendency to recruit and hire A+ players to join their team. These visionary individuals realize that their position of leadership and management is more important than their skill level at performing the routine functions of team members.

As a leader, and in order to lead an effective organization, you must understand that you can't do it all alone. If you're doing a majority of the work or if the team is critically dependent on your actual work functions, then the team is severely hampered. You're like the manager of a sports team. You might not be out there in the field with the rest of the team, but you know who needs to be in each specific position in order for your business to run like clockwork. One of the greatest attributes of true leaders is that they understand they can't know everything. They must know something about everything, but it's impossible to be a specialist in everything. Smart hiring means bringing in the right people with the skills and expertise that complement the missing pieces in the organization and the team they join.

FILLING IN THE PERFORMANCE GAPS

Businesses too often fail to recruit the right people to connect with customers; many organizations place just about anybody in the front-line customer service. The impact these people have on customers is too important to be left up to just anybody. Recruiting the right employee with the right personality, enthusiasm, drive, and interest in people most certainly demands more time and effort, especially if you intend to build an exceptional customer service team. This may, for example, be accomplished more effectively using personality profiles to identify the ideal applicants.

Managing the pool of customer-impacting skills within your organization is critical to maintain the momentum and consistency required to develop the type of experiences that matter to customers. Consistency is the critical catalyst to effective customer service. Just one day of great service won't be enough to create a lasting legacy. You'll have to string together day after day, week after week, month after month, until you have years of experience in serving before you'll truly begin to see the real impact of your service vision.

Management is a key component of maintaining lasting change and pushing the team toward excellence. But that doesn't mean you have to excel at customer service. What do you do when you're really not that good? Should you jump in the trenches with your people when you really aren't a star player? In reality, probably not. This doesn't mean you don't have your own strengths and talents, but what happens when you—the "boss"—start telling your employees how to do a task that you aren't all that great at yourself? Your team begins to resent you. This quickly erodes trust and respect in you as a leader and paves the way for chaos in the area—customer service—where organization is essential for ongoing success.

You've probably been an employee at some point. Haven't you ever had a boss, manager, or supervisor who told you how to do your job but never had a real understanding of how to best perform the duties that had been assigned to you? You probably did not like that they had no idea what it was like to be in your shoes—they just gave you orders without regard to how your duties were best performed.

Either you or people you know have likely said things akin to, "The boss is a jerk; he has no idea what it's like to do my job," or, "If the boss is gonna tell me what to do, he should first know how to do it himself." What's the point of all this? It's important for you to understand that you are not the best at everything in your business; therefore, you don't always have the best answers or advice to give every department you run.

You're the boss of multiple departments, and so you must fill those departments with people who are qualified to appropriately determine the best policies to have in place. You don't have to be the star; you just have to know how to find the right people to keep your business growing and running strong.

Rule 19

FORGET THE GOLDEN RULE

For those who don't know (though you probably do), the Golden Rule is, "Do unto others as you would have done unto you." This sounds wonderful in theory, and it is applicable in a general sense. We all want to be respected and treated with kindness, to have others praise us and acknowledge our skills and talents, but what about everything beyond that? You might think that there's not much beyond what I mentioned, which is why I'm inviting you to reconsider and keep reading.

JUST A MISUNDERSTANDING

Have you ever done something that, to you, felt innocent, but actually offended the other person you meant to be kind to? I was standing in line at the grocery store the other evening, holding a friendly conversation with the cashier. The woman in line behind me had wanted to join in on the conversation, so I was happy to have her as a part of it. The conversation went smoothly at first, and then the woman decided to make a joke that I found both derogatory and offensive.

I'm a professional in dealing with people—I didn't laugh at her joke, but I didn't belittle or criticize her. I realized that she thought she was doing something friendly, and she was treating me the way she would wish to be treated, telling me the type of joke that she would enjoy. I didn't enjoy the joke and I left matters peacefully, though imagine if it had been somebody else. Imagine if it had been you. Have you been in that situation where somebody has unintentionally offended you? Worse yet, have you been the person to offend someone else, when all you were doing was treating him or her the way you would prefer to be treated?

CHANGING UP THE "RULE"

Not all customers want to be treated the same. Just because you would like to have a nice conversation, getting to know your customers more deeply, it doesn't always mean they want the same. If you have a customer who places a strong emphasis on time, wanting only the facts and deadlines, you'd best give her what *she* wants, not what *you* want.

Here's a *new* rule to live by: Do unto others as *they* would have done unto *them*. Service isn't what you want from your customers. It's what your customers want from you. Don't make the mistake or run the risk of offending a customer by forcing your will onto an unsuspecting person. Not everyone likes what you like. Not everyone expects the same things you do. Delivering exceptional service means knowing how to make customers happy and delivering what customers expect from you.

This new principle of handling customers doesn't somehow invalidate the Golden Rule; the Golden Rule stands as a time-honored principle. Consider this principle to be the next step in the logical process of delivering your customers an exceptional experience that they'll remember was geared to what *they* wanted.

MAP A CLEAR JOURNEY TO GREAT CUSTOMER SERVICE

▶ Each day, your customer service team gets hundreds of emails from customers. These emails can range from basic username and password reset questions to complex requests and problems to solve. Some questions are easy and quick to answer. Others take time and effort as your service agents embark on a journey to find a solution.

Regardless of the nature of the customer's request, it's essential that you be clear on the plan for the customer and the ultimate experience result. Your customers aren't in the business of running your business. Your competitors would like to put you *out* of business. Unless you take control of the customer service journey and clearly define the outcomes that are right for you and your customers, someone else will take control for you, with potentially disastrous results.

THE CUSTOMER SERVICE JOURNEY
REQUIRES VISION

Your team must be dedicated to delivering an exceptional experience to every customer by helping each one know that they matter to you and that you will roll out the red carpet for them. But to do that, you have to know where you want to go. As a team, you must have vision. We all believe in creating the best service experience for our customers. We see each customer as a lifelong customer, not just a single sale. This means taking whatever time is needed to make sure we take care of the customer. You need a clear plan and a unified approach to customer service.

Step back and evaluate your customer service systems, processes, and practices. Are they fostering and encouraging collaboration with customers? Are they promoting solutions to customer problems? When you embark on a journey *with* the customer, you're much more likely to achieve the outcome you want. You'll begin to develop better customer relationships—the kind of relationships that build customer loyalty. You have the opportunity to go beyond what your customer experience has previously accomplished and to explore new ways of connecting with customers. Whether you're an organization that leads your industry in the customer service experience or an individual looking to optimize your ability to develop client relationships and inspire better team performance, taking advantage of this opportunity is entirely up to you. The ultimate destination—the type of customer service experience that connects people to you at the level of developing loyalty—is within your reach. Take the energy, enthusiasm, determination, and focus you currently have and step outside your comfort zone.

When you take that step forward, you begin the journey of exploration and welcome the challenge of the unknown; you will gain experience and knowledge through your work and the determination to overcome the obstacles you encounter. Persistent action in achieving a more excellent customer experience will allow you to reach new heights of excellence. There is no single path that leads there. Although the service actions are common, the ultimate experience and emotional connection you create with your customers is unique. The choice to discover and deliver it is entirely up to you.

THE CUSTOMER SERVICE JOURNEY REQUIRES CLARITY AND CONSISTENCY

You need focused preparation for how service should take place and clear objectives for what the end experience should be in order to consistently create positive connections in customer interactions. The lean startup movement has championed the bootstrappers, the shortcut takers, the minimum viable product, and the quick-to-market strategy. That rush to market may work in the race to deliver new services and capture early market share, but it will rarely work as a long-term strategy to engage customers and keep them happy. In the end, frustration and lack of complete cohesion between product and service will erode customer satisfaction and open the door to alternative solutions. Without consistency in your service execution, one-off customer experiences can cause confusion and foster disappointment in your customers. Creating the framework for consistent excellence in service is the key to long-term customer delight.

Without a clear vision and strategy for what your ultimate customer experience should be, you'll rarely end up with the consistent and concentrated effort needed in order to really make a difference to a majority of your customers. Are you 100 percent confident that every customer-impacting (not just customer-facing) team member understands the role he or she plays in the customer experience? Ask your people:

- Why you do what you do?
- What makes you better than other options?
- What's on the horizon that could steal away your customers?
- What's the level of urgency internally to strengthen what you offer and keep the customers you have?

A clear journey map is needed to align people, processes, services, and strategy in order to deliver desired customer behaviors and successful business outcomes.

Rule 21

DO A 60-SECOND CUSTOMER EXPERIENCE EVALUATION

▶ It's easy to get caught up in the day-to-day actions and forget to step back and see the big picture of customer experience. We often hear that we need to stop and evaluate, but if you're like me, you don't feel like you have time to stop. But reviewing *customer experience* is critical to maintaining focus on exceptional service. Luckily, you can take a short time to step back, review, and make plans for improving customer service and recharging the *customer experience*.

60 SECONDS TO LOYAL CUSTOMERS

In 60 seconds you can see exactly where you are in the customer experience journey, and how you're using customer service to develop loyal customers, by answering these simple questions.

`0:60` Is Customer Experience and Service Part of Your Business Culture?

Take a look around you right now. Do you see customer experience, customer service, and customer focus integrated into what you're doing right now? If you were to freeze time right now, would each individual in the organization be thinking about the customer experience? Acting with customer focus? This mentality determines if customer experience is part of your business culture.

Customer service and customer experience often become routine, day-to-day, go-through-the-motions actions. It's inevitable, since it's the essence of what you do. But even though working with customers is commonplace, it's crucial to the ongoing success of your organization. Each experience lays the groundwork for future relationships.

`0:50` Do You Have a Customer Experience Advantage?

When asked what we offer, or what we do, we typically begin long-winded explanations of business processes, service, or products. But are you communicating this effectively to your entire organization? Is your team consistent with your customer experience advantage? Can you break down your unique customer offering into a 1-minute pitch? How about 30 seconds? 15 seconds? 10 seconds? 5 seconds? Get the idea? Break down what you do and what you offer into long, medium, and short pitches. Communicate that value statement to everyone in your organization. Get people involved, committed, and connected with it.

`0:35` Is Customer Communication Part of Your Customer Experience?

Take a few seconds and look around at your team. How are they communicating with your customers? Are your customers able to reach you? Access information? Get resolution? Think of the touch points between your organization and your customer. Is your interaction satisfactory to your customers? Do your customers wish for more? Easier access? Better results? A 1-800 number and an IVR maze or phone queue isn't communication. These things frustrate customers. Effective customer experience involves having communication channels available to customers, with competent and qualified team members who can take action to meet customer needs.

`0:25` How Quickly Does Your Customer Service Respond to Customers?

We live in a digital age. We have instant Internet access, instant messaging, and instant coffee. So why do we still wait 20-plus minutes on hold when we call customer service? In our previous question, we talked about communication channels, but now we're digging down and evaluating those channels at meeting the needs and wants of customers. Are you doing that?

- Is your personal communication instant?
- How long are customers on hold on the phone before speaking to someone?
- How long do they wait before chatting?
- How long before their emails get a reply?
- How long do they search your site before they find the information they need?

`0:15` Do You Use Customer Service to Let Customers Know You Appreciate Them?

We live in a time when customers feel more and more ignored, when customer service is becoming more generic, impersonal, and robotic. What better way to differentiate yourself from the competition and set your customer experience apart from the crowd than by taking time to thank your customers? Don't have time? Me neither, but the time spent in thanking customers goes a long way to solidify the customer's relationship with your people and your brand.

Customers mean so much for any organization, but too many simply go unappreciated. Thanking customers is often absent from executive plans. Even when it's done, thanking customers seldom seems genuine. Stand out by making thanking customers a part of your operation. Make thanking customers part of your culture. Make thanking customers your competitive advantage.

`0:05` Does Your Customer Experience Include Customer Feedback?

Does it? Does it not? While it's the CEO who signs the paycheck, customers fund the business. Customers are the ultimate boss. Are you listening to what they have to say? Feedback isn't a right; it's a necessity. Getting and using feedback is critical to the customer experience. Be willing to listen, and most important, do something about the feedback you're given.

HOW DID YOU DO?

After these 60 seconds, you should have a good idea of how you're currently doing in implementing customer service to develop an exceptional customer experience that creates sustained growth and loyal customers. By answering these quick questions, you should now know what customer experience areas need development, what needs to be changed, and what you need to start doing to put the focus back on the customer.

Rule 22

DEVELOP 20/20 VISION FOR EXCEPTIONAL CUSTOMER SERVICE

▶ From integrating multichannel contact center strategy to developing the model for value-add and ROI to the organization and empowering employees to act in behalf of customers to develop the customer experience, managing the intricacies of customer service can be an extremely difficult challenge. The right insight, vision, and understanding are needed to develop a 20/20 clear vision for service experience at a macrolevel and in order to identify and orchestrate the individual components on the microlevel of service action.

Service leaders need to continually consider how they will benchmark their service delivery against competitor service offerings. How will testing be conducted to ensure that the right service levels are in place and that best practices are being implemented across the board within the organization? Leaders need to continually explore the latest developments in service channels, technologies, marketing, and thought leader insight in order to keep their organizations relevant with constantly shifting consumer demands.

The essence of great customer service and amazing customer experience is centered on establishing and maintaining the proper vision of service. The customer service vision banner has to be bold and held up high so that *all individuals in the organization can see your service message at all times.* You've got to see the big picture first, then make sure that your team sees *that same* big picture. The top organizations today are finding new and more innovative ways to build competitive service offerings and provide differentiation in the development of the customer relationship.

OPEN YOUR EYES TO WHAT
CUSTOMERS NEED TODAY

Managing excellent customer service and developing amazing customer experiences require keeping your eyes wide-open to the *current* needs and wants of your customers. Is the customer being delighted and wowed today? Is the service being provided meeting and exceeding customer expectations? Are you providing all of the tools, information, and services that create the best experience for the customer?

Today's digitally connected customers have access to more information than ever before. They simply expect more from the brands and organizations with which they interact on a daily basis. Customers know about the resources that organizations have at their disposal and the communication channels that are readily available. They expect organizations today to be more loyalty-focused and to go further in connecting with and serving customers. Customers today know that they are "always right." Even when they are wrong, they expect today's smart organizations to compensate and find a way to deliver an exceptional service experience.

OPEN YOUR EYES TO WHAT CUSTOMERS
WILL NEED TOMORROW

Managing excellent customer service and developing amazing customer experiences also require keeping your eyes wide-open to the *future* needs and wants of the customer. I see a lot of talk about customer service and dealing with angry and upset customers. There are plenty of reports on customers' dissatisfaction with service providers. Why? Where's the disconnect? Service providers don't go out there trying to be bad at servicing customers. I think the real problem is that customer service today is too reactive and not sufficiently proactive.

In order to remain relevant to today's customers, organizations have to aim beyond the traditional customer service approaches. You'll need to do more than just show up in order to win the customer today. This means going above and beyond the traditional deliverables of upselling and overall satisfaction in the contact center. Today's customer experience demands are emotional, and customers expect personal connection and personalized service in each interaction. The demands on today's service organizations have gone beyond just service, and instead are focused on reaching the level of consultancy and advocacy on behalf of the customer.

BECOME A CUSTOMER ADVOCATE

Developing your role as a customer advocate should be the ultimate goal. When you are a trusted adviser, it becomes much more difficult for the customer to consider alternate service providers. The choice then isn't just about picking from another set of options, but is more intricate as the new service provider must meet a much higher level of service delivery in order to truly offer added value to the customer. My colleague and customer experience visionary Shep Hyken has a concept he teaches when he encourages organizations to create *demanding customers*. As you increase the demands of your customers, it sets the bar much higher for competitors to reach in order to take away your customers. Even if customers were to switch, they would probably quickly realize how much they really had while working with you. Make yourself so good that customers can't bear to live without you.

Awesome customer service managers and teams are visionary. True customer advocates see beyond the individual customer transaction and continually envision the full value of the lifetime loyalty of the customer. Service leaders must always be brainstorming new and innovative ways to connect with customers in order to take service to a new level. The really great teams are always looking for feedback and then doing something about it. In the customer feedback, special emphasis is put on what customers want from the organization, how their experience was, and what points within the process they felt were troublesome.

ACCEPT THAT YOU CAN'T PLEASE EVERYONE

▶ Despite your best efforts to deliver exceptionally great customer service, some customers refuse to be content even when they're given the best service you can offer. It's a reality in life that no matter how hard you try, some people just won't be satisfied. There's no point in trying to be everything to everyone—especially those who will refuse to see your best as good enough.

When customers work with service teams, they generally get what they ask for. Service agents know what information the customers need and are helpful and pleasant during the interaction. So why do the numbers show that customer service continues to suffer? Why are service ratings still lagging and customers still complaining about service? That's a tough question to answer, but all you can do is do your best in every service interaction. If that's not good enough, so be it.

ACTING WHEN A CUSTOMER REFUSES TO BE SATISFIED WITH YOUR SERVICE

Don't think that it can't happen to you. There will always be customers with bad attitudes, those who just can't seem to appreciate things, who want more even when they don't deserve it. But being able to rise above the forces outside your control is critical in order to persist through the process of developing your service experience. So stop trying to please everybody and start trying to live your service vision to the fullest.

The angry customers will continue to remain angry. As long as you've done everything reasonably in your power to serve them, you should stop stressing about it. Attempting to please every single person will eventually dampen your desire to serve. You just can't give enough when the individual on the other side refuses to be satisfied. Instead of living with regrets of unattainable satisfaction, focus your time on creating new opportunities and being authentic in those interactions. One or two bad reviews weighed against hundreds of positive reviews is proof you're on the right track for great service. Learn from the bad reviews, but don't let them linger and prevent you from achieving great service results.

PROVIDING THE CORE VALUES OF SERVICE

The key to overcoming the naysayers is to emphasize the core values of service that each customer deserves:

- Perspective
- Courtesy
- Gentility
- Consideration
- Patience

Beyond that, it's up to the customer to bring to the table similar characteristics on the receiving end of the service interaction. The type of customers you want maintain perspective in the midst of their problem. They realize that the same courtesy extended to them should be returned to the agent serving them. These customers can act with gentility and consideration of the efforts being made by service agents. Valuable customers are patient. They understand that problems are frustrating, but they can also recognize the efforts of agents working to make things right.

SOLVING REAL CUSTOMER SERVICE ISSUES

When customers can't be pleased, customer service shouldn't be the first to be blamed. It's true that communication won't always be perfect. Hindsight is 20/20, and some actions taken might not have been the best choice, given the real issue the customer faces. But overreacting only cripples those involved in the current problem and affects their ability to make effective decisions in future service interactions. Ultimately, the emphasis needs to be on ensuring that you give the customer options, deliver results, and make a difference.

Accept that things won't always go right, but be sure that you're always right about the big picture of how service should work. Measure your service experience against the reasonable expectations of the customers you service in order to determine your success in developing effective experiences and managing the needs of customers.

Rule 24

SEE YOURSELF AS A CUSTOMER SERVICE LEADER

Not all leaders are bosses, and not all bosses are great leaders. There are distinct differences between leaders who inspire men and women to achieve astounding results and bosses who maintain business operations. Unfortunately, in this fast-paced and money-driven world of competition, the "boss" has pretty much stopped being a leader as such and has become more the person at the top who issues instructions with the understanding that they will be followed implicitly. This kind of atmosphere results in companies full of unhappy employees, no longer working to improve the business but just putting in an appearance to receive their paycheck at the end of the week, or, alternatively, to fight it out with other disgruntled staff members to take over as boss so they can have their turn at dishing out the orders.

This kind of attitude in a workplace is damaging to a business because basically everyone is working under duress to reach the goals and targets of the company. It's a lot more profitable and healthier for all people involved if companies employ and nurture leaders, who fulfill their role through leading by example, taking the pole position, and sharing that position with his or her staff members. The biggest difference between a boss and a leader seems to be that a boss creates internal squabbling, disharmony, and reluctance, thereby making reaching targets difficult, while leaders inspire pride, encouragement, and cooperation, driving the business to reach and usually surpass its goals.

"BOSS" CHARACTERISTICS

Unfortunately the word *boss* has negative connotations. We think of someone in charge, giving orders, demanding compliance in a domineering manner. Bosses are taking orders from higher-ups, so they need their staff to perform in order to maintain appearances, and to protect their own position. Usually having to work within a specific budget, a boss will demand extra work for less pay in order to fulfill business goals.

People working under the boss will often work harder and longer for fear of losing their jobs. What the boss says goes, so not performing to standards set by the boss places staff in a very precarious situation. Respect is expected, simply because he's the boss, and for no other reason; certainly not because it's been earned. Employees understand that for job security they must conform, regardless of their own personal feelings about their position, their boss, or the company they work for.

LEADER CHARACTERISTICS

A leader must be a great manager (or boss) but also know how to lead in a positive manner. Leaders are more likely to influence someone to want to work for them, because they lead by their own example. A leader will have a great work ethic, which will be obvious to other staff members. Basically, a leader leads, whereas a boss gives orders. People working with a leader are usually more inspired and encouraged and happy to follow directions. A leader provides a positive example, clear guidelines, constructive criticism, or appreciation for a job well done, all of which strengthen the whole team.

Possibly the biggest advantage of having a team leader is that employees feel like they are part of the whole. Employees are encouraged to offer ideas or suggestions, become involved in business discussions, and show initiative. They're also encouraged to be able to work unsupervised.

WHO WOULD YOU RATHER BE?

Are you a boss or a leader? Both positions can exert influence because of the authority placed on the position. But only one earns respect and trust by setting a great example. Being a boss is isolating. Leadership, conversely, is collaborative. A leader understands that it's a joint effort among team members that creates success. Leaders instill pride in their workforce and build confidence; team members know they're critical components of the whole group.

Leaders inspire team members and cultivate their talents and skills to increase productivity and success. Bosses squeeze work out of people, which often stifles creativity and, eventually, productivity. It stands to reason that employees who are being led are more productive, happier, and more creative than those who are performing on demand. For any company to thrive and move forward in the business world, it must have the full effort, cooperation, and energy of its employees. Success is the common goal of all concerned.

You can easily see why a great customer service team needs a leader, not a boss. When you see yourself as a customer service leader and act accordingly, team members will perform at the top of their game, confident in their ability to provide the best service to your customers, rather than just show up at work every day to claim a paycheck.

USE POSITIVE WORDS TO WIN CUSTOMERS

▶ The way you express yourself in your customer service interactions will determine whether customers receive your message in a positive or negative way. Communication is at the core of successful customer service. And language is a powerful tool when it comes to how communication works. Even when you're conveying unpleasant news, the impact can be softened by the use of what we call positive language.

Negative language and communication doesn't necessarily mean a negative attitude. Even those stellar team members with positive attitudes can use language that creates the impression of negativity for your customers. Falling into the trap of negative talk is easy. Too many of us do it without even thinking about it, especially when we write to others. A poor selection of words is enough to make a negative customer interaction, sour the customer relationship, and contribute to a poor customer experience.

TYPICAL EXPERIENCE

"We regret to inform you that we cannot process your application to register your business name, since you have neglected to provide sufficient information. Please complete ALL sections of the attached form and return it to us."

Is it polite? Certainly. But it's also overly formal, and depressing with too many negative words. Words like "cannot" and "neglected" focus on barriers to your customer and place blame, leading to a poor service experience. Can a typical interaction like this be improved to create a winning customer experience?

EXCEPTIONAL EXPERIENCE

"Congratulations on your new business name!

To complete your registration, I'll just need some additional details from you. Could you return the attached with the highlighted areas filled in? I'll then be able to complete the remaining steps and send your certificate within two weeks.

Good luck in your business! I wish you much success."

This is personal and positive, even when asking for additional details. What customer wouldn't come away from this interaction full of confidence, excitement, and willingness to complete the required items?

- Positive customer service language focuses on *actions* that can be done.
- Positive customer service language offers *choices* instead of roadblocks.
- Positive customer service language is *helpful* and *encouraging*.
- Positive customer service language includes *positive consequences* that can be expected.
- Positive customer service language is *timely* and *time-bound* so customers know when to expect service results.

Language can make or break your customer service experience. Positive language is the key to improved customer relationships. Take a look at your recent customer service interactions. Is the language used in your emails or phone calls contributing to a positive customer service experience?

A great customer experience happens when great service takes place. For us to be able to deliver exceptional customer experiences, it's essential that we correctly understand the nature of customer experience, customer service, and customers themselves. Using the right words to connect with customers is critical in order for you to excel in customer experience and master your customer relationships.

LEARN TO DEAL WITH FULFILLMENT PROBLEMS

▶ Sadly, like rain at a barbecue, fulfillment problems are sometimes unavoidable, and they can cause a lot of damage. Losing customer trust, denting your reputation, and impacting sales—you know how harmful order mistakes can be to your business. In an ideal world, fulfillment strategies (unlike a hastily erected party tarpaulin) would be watertight. Unfortunately, due to human error and system mistakes, such as ineffective forecasting, customer orders still go wrong on occasion, no matter how hard you try to avoid mistakes. Anticipating potential customer order fulfillment problems can limit the damage and transform adversity into opportunity.

MAKE SURE TO KEEP CUSTOMERS IN THE LOOP

If you quickly update customers and inform them that things aren't going entirely to plan, you lessen the potential shock, anger, and mistrust that poor order fulfillment can bring. For this reason, effective communication (from stating initial order/transaction confirmations to sending dispatch/delivery notifications) is invaluable. In addition to allowing the entire fulfillment process to run seamlessly, communications prevent escalating or surprise issues by highlighting problems early and providing regular situational updates.

If a mistake is genuinely your fault, you should immediately accept the blame and sincerely apologize for it. Sincerity is key—if you don't appear truly sorry, your customers will notice and your nonchalance will aggravate them further. When order errors occur, customers want to know why. To reassure them that similar problems will not reoccur in the future and to identify and correct root causes yourself, you must be able to provide a solid reason for inefficient service.

SHOW YOU CARE BY LISTENING
AND BEING AVAILABLE

Ideally, if customer orders go wrong (stock runs out, deliveries are misplaced, etc.), you will know first and should notify the customer. However, this is not always possible, meaning customers will contact you to make complaints. In such situations, being rapidly and easily available via all communications channels is necessary to salvage customer trust and prove you care. Good customer service is integral to limiting potential damage to your business. So train your staff well to show compassion, *listen* to customer issues, and again, apologize on behalf of the company, accepting blame sincerely when necessary.

READILY OFFER ADEQUATE COMPENSATION

Along with sincere apologies and effective customer service when problems occur, you should offer compensatory gestures or tokens, however small. Consolations will vary depending on the severity of the issue, but are used to prove to customers that you appreciate their business and you want their continued loyalty. Compensation should not require additional customer spending. For example, money-off vouchers may antagonize customers already poised to walk away from your services rather than entice them back in. In such circumstances, reimbursement or an offer of free services may be a better gesture.

REVIEW EXISTING CUSTOMER
FULFILLMENT PROCESSES

Of course, if mistakes keep occurring (say orders are inexplicably incorrect, repeatedly late, or disappear entirely), it's important to investigate who or what is really at fault. You may need to alter aspects of your supply chain and fulfillment strategy, or provide better training for your staff. So review to improve, but be prepared for the occasional spot of stormy weather.

▸ Show you care and listen by accepting blame and apologizing sincerely.
▸ Always try to provide a reason for service errors and mistakes.
▸ Offer adequate compensation.
▸ Investigate the cause of the original problem—your supply chain, fulfillment strategy, or training schemes may need adjusting.

REPEAT, REPEAT, REPEAT, AND THEN REPEAT AGAIN, WITH PURPOSE

▶ In order to establish a pattern of great customer service, your people require frequent exposure to great experiences. We repeat these patterns over and over again so that even when we don't feel 100 percent engaged, they naturally take place when, where, and how they should. By repetition, good customer service actions become habits and, eventually, natural behavior. Behavior is how one automatically acts in response to situations or circumstances.

Simplify the process of learning and acting out those positive customer actions. Make it clear to everyone involved in the customer interaction what the proper mechanics of these actions are and what the desired outcomes should be. Encourage frequent repetition of actions and visualization of the desired results. With effective training and consistent practice, delivering great customer experience can be part of our natural behavior when we're involved in any customer interaction.

REPETITION WITH PURPOSE

It's in the nature of customer service to repeat, repeat, and repeat again. From greetings and good-byes to the questions service agents answer for customers, there's going to be repetition on the contact center; there's no way around it. But the words you choose to use today, proven words that have been used time after time in previous customer interactions, have real power in developing the type of service experience and customer relationship that could mean the difference for the success of your organization. Sure, the words are the same as before, but is the desire to provide excellent service still as present as it should be?

When a task becomes repetitious, there's a tendency to take it for granted. Consider phrases as simple as, "If there's anything else I can do to help, please let me know." Or, "If you have any other questions, please let me know." They are two of the most often used customer service statements, but is there real meaning in the words you choose to say each day? Do your customers really feel your desire to serve? Do you back up what you say by actually jumping at the chance to serve customers when they take you up on your offer? When there's real *purpose* behind the repetitive tasks performed in the service of customers, service becomes more than just fixing problems. Behind every customer question or problem there's a real individual with needs, wants, and desires. Do customers actually feel your desire to serve? Can they sense the meaning behind the repetitive tasks you're performing today? Your attention to detail in service and the speed with which you act on a customer's request show customers your level of commitment to making life better for them.

THE POWER OF REPETITION

Becoming persuasive and effective in customer service and communication won't come naturally at first. It will take time, attention, and effort. The strategies and techniques used in writing and speaking for service can be extremely effective in developing the right customer experience that differentiates your organization from the competition. Repetition is the process through which you develop those skills and techniques, testing and refining the actions performed until they yield the optimal result for the customer. The wise karate master reminds his students that they shouldn't be afraid of the 10,000 strikes practiced only once, but of the one strike that has been practiced 10,000 times. In order to master your actions and achieve the maximum positive result from your efforts, you're going to have to practice, and practice means repeating, over and over again. Through repetition, we learn how and when to apply our words and actions in order to receive the most effective result. This means mastering the ability to:

- Deliver the right message.
- Deliver the message at the right time.
- Deliver in the most efficient way for the customer.
- Deliver with emotion, so there's a residual effect from service.
- Deliver enough residual effect over time so that a relationship is developed.

Daily repetition makes a task progressively easier. This just makes sense. Do you see successful athletes who train only once a month? Repetition is a natural learning process. Through purposeful repetition we develop actions, habits, and, ultimately, character. Repetition for the sake of repetition simply leads to compulsion, which is devoid of meaning. Repetition with purpose enables you to capitalize on daily tasks and unlock exceptional results.

ELIMINATE THREE WORDS FROM YOUR VOCABULARY

▶ Millions of words are used each day in customer service communication. However, three little words can create a trap that can easily destroy the positive customer experience you're hoping to establish. Problems naturally happen. Dealing with problems is part of the service experience. While it may not be your fault, make the issue your problem to solve. The key to great service is more effective service actions and the ability to effectively communicate with customers.

AVOID THESE THREE WORDS

Think before ever using these three words and try to avoid them at all cost.

"Busy"

"All of our agents are currently busy." What you're really saying is: "We're too busy for you." *Busy* is often used to generate sympathy, but in service communication, *busy* simply means unwilling, unable, and don't care.

The fix? Prioritize. Be more efficient. Be more effective at finding answers, resolutions, and preemptively solving potential customer issues before they happen. Anticipate the possibilities and create systems to help customers before they get stuck, become frustrated, and flood your customer service team with help requests.

"But"

Anytime you use *but* in any type of customer service communication you completely erase whatever positive words may have been previously spoken. *But* means "can't" or "won't." In customer service, *but* is telling the customer a big fat "*no*." Make absolute statements about what *can* be done. Even when the solution involves something from the customer, state options, not excuses as to why things can't be done.

"Blame"

Blame for why things can't be done is always plentiful. There are always enough excuses for why something can't be done, why something went wrong, and who is at fault. But placing blame is the last thing that customers really want to hear. Blame prevents you from seeing the real problem. Blame isn't a fix. Blame isn't an answer. Blame isn't a solution.

CHANGE THE WAY YOU COMMUNICATE

Effective customer service communication isn't about identifying problems; it's about offering solutions. Customers don't care who caused the problem. Customers care little if you confirm that something indeed is wrong. What matters is what's being done to resolve the problem and how quickly they can get back to doing what they need to get done.

Certainly you can't completely banish the three little words from your vocabulary; that's just silly. Some organizations miss the point and simply substitute similar words that perpetuate ineffective customer service. Beware of the meaning behind "busy," "but," and "blame," and your customer service communication will develop better, more effective customer relationships.

Rule 29

BE LOVABLE TO YOUR CUSTOMERS

▶ Regardless of what you offer to your customers, success will largely be determined by your ability to create value for your customers, and then repeat that process over and over again for many more customers. Really making a difference for your customers in the long run is more than just providing a product or service. It's about evoking real emotions that customers experience time and time again as they use your product and service.

Love it or hate it, Apple's product experience is unsurpassed. Other pieces of technology are more advanced, but Apple offers the experience of working with a product as beautiful as it is functional. Jeffrey Kluger writing for *Time* magazine says that the secret behind Apple is the ability to create a "desirability of Apple products on an almost cellular level."[1] That type of emotional connection reaches an almost spiritual level. It can't be done by simply adding more features. If you want to create that same level of engagement, you have to develop a unique experience that customers can't get anywhere else.

COURT YOUR CUSTOMERS

If you want your customers to buy from you, you'll have to bring out your best and really court your customer—yes, court your customer. When customers "fall in love" with you, they'll overlook your faults and see the good in you. That level of relationship endures; people think twice before choosing to turn away to another service provider. And that level of relationship goes both ways. As you learn to love your customers for who they really are, you'll overlook their faults, see their true value, and make decisions in the best interest of their welfare. This two-way connection between you and your customers is what creates customer loyalty. Creating that special connection with your customers isn't just about your outward actions. It requires real emotion, feeling, and the desire to do things for the other person.

Whether winning new customers or keeping your valuable customers, there's a real ripple effect of great brand design and exceptionally crafted customer experiences. The key is *if* customers believe that you can really deliver what they want most. Think of all the choices, constant campaigning, and advertising that your competitors throw at your customers every day. When it comes down to it, your customers don't simply purchase from you because of logic, but because of emotion. They care about the connection they have with you and expect you to deliver it time and time again.

SERVICE IS THE KEY TO A CUSTOMER'S HEART

Customers fall in love with or hate brands because of customer service. Customers buy or don't buy based on how they feel they're being treated. Customers go out of their way for a special connection with a brand. And customers call it quits when brands neglect them and fail to deliver what they need and want. Making customers happy doesn't mean giving everything away for free. And it's not something that only a select few organizations with insane customer service budgets can do. Just focus on these six keys ways to make your customers fall in love with what you do.

1. Deliver awesome service with awesome value.
2. Make sure your product or service is at its best.
3. Create interesting, engaging content that matters.
4. Participate in interesting, engaging conversations that matter to your customers.
5. Overdeliver on your promises.
6. Encourage feedback, do something about it, and then let the customer know what you've done.

BE AT YOUR BEST

Ensure that every individual you recruit for your customer service efforts is at his or her best. Empower the people who serve to do their best for the customer and empower customers to get the most from what you offer. Make service more than just completing a transaction. Go above and beyond by instructing and imparting new knowledge to your customers in order for them to become better at what they do. Filter through the endless amount of data available and focus on the key metrics that ultimately enable you to provide the type of service that your customers deserve. Step outside your own circle and join the community of customers, professionals, and thought leaders. Contribute to the development of your field and show customers that you're invested in what you do beyond just generating a sale.

Your customers can be your greatest source of happiness as they help your organization make its goals and achieve greater success. Customers don't want to do business begrudgingly; if they do, it'll only be for a short time. Frustrated and disappointed customers will eventually find an alternative and leave you out in the cold. In order to win customers and keep winning their business, you have to be at your best and show them you care. When you truly care about customers and back it up with your actions, customers can't help but fall in love with you.

CURE YOURSELF OF THE "BETWEEN 11 AND 5" SYNDROME

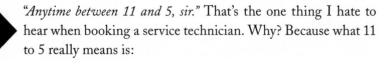

"Anytime between 11 and 5, sir." That's the one thing I hate to hear when booking a service technician. Why? Because what 11 to 5 really means is:

A) Miss a day of work and aggravate my boss.
B) Ask my neighbor to help out, get stuck in awkward small talk about the weather, and return the favor by mowing his lawn next Saturday afternoon.
C) My least preferred option: Go to work, miss the technician, and start all over again with the first two options.

The first impression you get from a service provider that has just given you the dreaded "between 11 and 5" slogan is a bad one. The speed of the response sets the tone for how customers feel service providers view their customers. One of the biggest reasons for customer churn is the lack of available support when customers need service providers the most. A company that fails to commit to and achieve a short service action time is a company pushing its customers straight to the competition. With today's advances in technology, customers expect real-time updates and more accurate predictions of when service will happen. Instant service may not always be available, but service accuracy is certainly expected.

Here are a few tips for service businesses looking to tighten their appointment windows, improve service timeliness, and keep their customers for a long, long time.

CREATE MOBILITY FROM MOBILE

Having the field team connected to the back office and dispatchers in real time is a sure way to deliver more reliable appointment slots. With a mobile workforce management solution, the field team can send live updates and chat in context with the office and colleagues. Managers and dispatchers can quickly reschedule technicians and tasks based on up-to-the-second information from the field. If one technician is delayed, another technician can be located and immediately sent in his place. The service appointment is kept, the customer is happy, and your service business will continue to grow.

STOP PING-PONG SERVICE

A first-time fix is what every service company should be aiming for. That means you need a good scheduling solution that will automatically schedule the right person with the right skill set and the right equipment for the job. By taking into consideration all the variables such as employee skills, preferences, location, and assets needed, service businesses can increase their first-time fix rates almost overnight. And what better way to end a service call than telling your customer, "Everything is fixed, ma'am. There's no need for me to come back!"

PUT CUSTOMERS IN CONTROL

In the service industry, the customer is boss. Make him feel it by putting the power of appointment booking in his own hands. Online appointment booking cuts out needless waiting on the phone by allowing the customer to conveniently select and change a delivery time to suit his own schedule. Customers can let you know how they prefer to be updated, whether it's through social media channels such as Facebook, automated texts, or a phone call to their mobile device. All of these options allow the customer to be in the driver's seat and feel more connected to the service he is receiving.

MANAGE CUSTOMER EXPECTATIONS
IN A 24/7 WORLD

Technology is often misinterpreted as the solution to service problems. If you think of technology as the solution, you'll be disappointed to see the burden of service actually increase instead. Technology is simply a building block of the service experience. How you choose to incorporate it will determine the level of service experience you provide to your customers. Technology often arrives at a faster pace than we can fully comprehend its usefulness and effectively apply it.

Much of the service disconnect today happens because organizations haven't aligned the possibilities of technology with the operations frameworks for improved service. Effectively utilized, technology can extend your ability to reach and serve customers. Technology efficiencies can bridge the gap between constraints of service resources and customer expectations, enhancing the customer experience. However, racing headlong into using new technology before you or your people are fully aware of how and where it can be applied can create more customer service problems than it solves.

As you understand who you are, your capabilities, your customers, and the expectations of service, you'll be able to establish the right framework for proper communication and deliver the service that customers want. Make sure customers remain informed and feel in control; create the right structure for effective service to take place; and take advantage of available technology to extend your ability to deliver what your customers want.

DON'T RUSH TECHNOLOGY TO FIX SERVICE PROBLEMS

For too many organizations, the call center is failing to deliver the service experience that customers expect. Simply adding more technology won't fix the ills of today's call center. Technology is never the solution. Technology enables more efficient and effective processes that can create the right customer service experience customers expect. But rushing new technology before making sure it's the right fit can be worse than adding no technology at all. You've got to start with the customer experience and work backward to the technology. You can't start with the technology and try to figure out where you're going to try to incorporate it into your customer service experience. Technology alone isn't enough to differentiate the service offered by your organization from that of the competition. It's how the technology is utilized. Does it truly make the service experience better for your customers?

In trying to get the customer service experience right, technology, for the sake of technology alone, is not greater than the sum of its parts. It's only when you have a crystal clear focus on what the experience should be and the difference you want to make in the life of your customers that the right technology, properly applied, becomes real innovation that transforms the way business is done.

As new technology becomes available, there comes with it the risk of attempting to take advantage of it right away in order to get the jump on your competitors. But rushing technology without the proper plan to incorporate it into the service experience will only disrupt the process that customers are used to and create disjointed experiences and chaos in service. Research has to be done and data must be carefully analyzed and incorporated into an actual strategy for opportunities to yield the greatest results.

It's easy to see why people rush. Being able to offer the latest to customers can be the deciding factor between becoming a leader or being unknown. The challenge, however, is that changes to the customer interaction create disruption to processes and customer flow. Unless customers instantly begin to see real value from the added technology, it's more likely that customers will see the addition as a nuisance and miss out on developing the satisfying experience.

Apple is clearly focused on its processes and products. Apple knows who it is, understands the needs of its customers, and has a clear vision for the customer experience it wants its customers to have. Apple sticks with its game plan and is very patient as its processes develop.

Customer experience can't be rushed. In order for you to capitalize on the opportunities that exist for you and your organization, your processes will need to be carefully crafted and then executed to perfection, over and over again. Without this type of focus, simply adding the latest tools or service is a gamble, one that you can't afford to make. Technology alone is not enough to make the difference you need in order to win the customer today and keep customers around tomorrow.

Rule 32

EMBRACE YOUR SERVICE IMPERFECTIONS

▶ The ancient Japanese philosophy of Wabi Sabi encourages individuals to celebrate imperfections and find the beauty in the natural processes around us. Wabi Sabi, rooted particularly in the ancient tea ceremony, emphasizes prized handmade bowls that are often unevenly glazed, irregularly shaped, and at times even cracked from long years of wear. In the face of unmistakable flaws of this type, Wabi Sabi teaches us to overlook such shortcomings and appreciate what we've been given today.

Customer service is never perfect. There's always something you can do better, and the experience can always be improved. Customer service is an intensely human experience, and humans are imperfect. Maintaining the proper perspective in terms of the right outcomes from service is key in order to continue making progress in customer service. No matter how much you try and how long you train them, people will make mistakes. The sooner you learn to embrace the reality of imperfection, the sooner you can free your mind to see the ultimate goal of creating the type of service your customers want. Developing this positive mentality is critical for those who oversee service work. It's not easy, but it's worth it in order to see the possibilities once you learn to overcome the mistakes that will come.

CUSTOMER SERVICE MISTAKES HAPPEN

Nobody ever wakes up hoping to have a service disaster that day. It just happens—and it happens to all of us. Keep in mind that service requires human interaction, and humans make mistakes. It's easier to stay motivated if you can consistently look past the minor faults of those who serve. Stay positive and remember that there's hardly ever going to be a day when some mistake isn't made or when something doesn't go wrong. Embrace those imperfections and look for the positive. Use mistakes as opportunities to test your processes and your resolve to deliver the ultimate service experience that your customers deserve.

Even companies known for their excellent customer service make mistakes. If you search for reviews online, you're guaranteed to find some upset Amazon customers. Research Zappos reviews, and you'll see that their legendary service isn't always perfect. Starbucks baristas get orders wrong. Apple products sometimes break. No company's service experience is flawless, and yours won't be, either. How you choose to view imperfections, and your attitude toward overcoming your shortcomings, can mean a world of a difference when it comes to the ultimate experience and service results.

HOW WILL YOU MEASURE YOURSELF?

Most mistakes made each day are beyond your control. What you can control is your reaction to the mistakes and your resolve to learn from them and improve processes and workflows in order to overcome such mistakes. Whether you explode in rage and make matters worse, or stay in control and learn from the experience, is up to you. Neither reaction will erase the mistake, but how you react can set the tone for the ultimate result.

Good people make mistakes. Great leaders allow them to make them. While allowing for risks to be taken and mistakes to be made can be scary for those who are responsible for the experience, it's in the process of learning from the mistakes that those involved in service ultimately grow. True leaders, those who develop the transformational processes leading to exceptional change, embrace the natural imperfections of service, rely on their own courage, and encourage others to develop it themselves in order to improve service. It's then that you see the true power of the learning opportunity that mistakes present. Use mistakes as opportunities to mentor and coach those who haven't yet perfected their skills as they work toward achieving top-notch customer service.

ACCEPT THAT YOU WILL FAIL

In order to master something, you have to first begin to do it. Realistically, your first time doing anything, you will make mistakes. What every customer service blogger, consultant, speaker, writer, and software provider *won't* tell you is that it's OK to make mistakes in customer service. I don't mean constantly making mistakes, but part of the mastering process means sometimes failing while you work to perfect your skills. Getting to the point where customer service is good, or even great, takes time, energy, and consistent effort.

Give yourself permission to fail while you learn the intricacies of how to master service. As you continue to learn and work through the process of developing yourself, you'll slowly begin to work out your service flaws, and eventually perfect service will emerge. Seeing the development of greatness is one of the most fulfilling aspects of the learning process. No one will master something on the first try; that's just not realistic. The sooner you realize and learn to accept the fact that bad is natural at the start, but can be overcome, the closer you'll be toward developing greatness in your service experience.

It's easy to be held back by the fear of failure or worrying that others won't see what you know you eventually will be able to do. But when you're trying to create something great, doubt from others and lack of support are part of the process. You have to fail and fail fast as you work toward finding out what works and how it works best. In reality, it's OK to be bad; it's necessary to be bad before you can ever be good and eventually great at something.

NEVER COMPROMISE ON CUSTOMER FOCUS

Most of us will spin our wheels at first. It takes time before we really get the hang of what we're doing and find that groove of doing it right. But as we focus on treating customers like royalty, even as we move, it seems, from one mistake to another, those customers will begin to see us for who we are. Maybe not all of them will stick it out, but most will, and the relationship you will develop on the way to success will be magical.

CUSTOMERS ARE NOT ALWAYS RIGHT, BUT THEY ARE ALWAYS CUSTOMERS

▶ This is such a predicament for people in the hospitality industry. What do you do as a customer service professional when the customer is obviously wrong? Sometimes customers jump to conclusions and they're just plain wrong! To make my point, I'd like to tell you about an embarrassing moment of mine, when, as a customer, I did that very thing.

I was in South Jordan, Utah, with a group of people in a beautiful little restaurant. Toward the end of what had been a wonderful meal, the service manager stopped at our table and asked if we were happy with our meals and the service provided. As it's my job to offer and share my advice on service-related matters, I took it upon myself to offer this lovely restaurant some of my highly prized advice—for free!

"Everything was really delightful; however I thought the sauce was possibly a little spicier than it should be." The manager didn't bat an eyelid. With a friendly but deadpan face she said: "You're absolutely right, sir. I totally agree that the Insanity Fire Sauce is pretty spicy."

Sadly (for me), I had never even seen the menu, due to the fact that I was a little late in arriving at our table and the other guests had already ordered for the table. So the value of my "highly prized" advice turned out to be precisely what it cost the restaurant—nothing at all! Zero—zilch—nada!

Her response was a most gracious and hospitable way of saying, "You, as our valued customer, are right," but what she was also saying was, "Perhaps next time you might read the menu before you make a complaint, and save yourself from having to suffer unnecessary discomfort."

CUSTOMERS ARE OFTEN WRONG

It seems to be human nature to go off half-cocked with incomplete information and start making accusations. Of course, being human means that no two people see the same thing in exactly the same way, and this includes customers and their often-imperfect views of situations and, yes, spicy food. Most customers are not really aware of the particular button that's been pushed to create their complaint, and they certainly don't accept any responsibility for making the complaint. They also don't consider your limited powers as a service provider and appear to deliberately misread your position and your duties. Many customers like to get on their high horse and stand on principle—their principle, of course. They often forget what their initial irritation was, in an attempt to protect their egos and to prove themselves right. Basically, everything gets thrown way out of proportion compared to what the issue actually was.

When the customer is obviously wrong, where does your responsibility begin? You're the person on the other end of the phone, the other side of the desk, the one who serves customers. Because you also are human, your perspective on any situation is also going to be flawed. You're made aware of what your customer is concerned about, whether they're right or wrong. Now you must handle this situation in a "customer service" kind of way, without your own views and opinions entering the argument. You have to determine in a "the-customer-is-always-right" manner just how the blame and responsibility for resolving this situation should be handled.

Again, because you're human, this can be a very difficult situation to handle. We've all been in the situation where we really want to embarrass or vilify a particular customer solely because a previous customer annoyed us, or got the better of us in some way. Perhaps the customer reminds you of someone you don't particularly like. And what about when you're handling a phone matter and you desperately need that bathroom break? We've all been there, where we get rid of the potential customer as quickly as possible because we have more pressing matters of our own.

FOCUS ON THE PROBLEM, NOT THE CUSTOMER

Maintaining the focus on the customer's ultimate end-to-end journey and experience can only be done by eliminating negative emotions that naturally develop when customers are wrong or when things go wrong during the customer interaction. When you learn to see the customer not as a problem but as a positive reward and the customer's problem as a barrier to retaining the reward, then you'll come to understand the true nature of service and the reason why you serve customers. Sustaining this point of view helps overcome the imperfect human element of service that allows problems to create enmity between customers and those who serve them.

Rather than seeing the customer as a personal challenge to you, the agent, realize that the customer is a partner and the problem is the challenge. That kind of mindset is how successful organizations enjoy consistent long-term customer loyalty and retain their customers year after year.

Instead of arguing over who is right and who is wrong, the only real choice is doing what you can to keep the customer. Customers are frequently wrong; they're often upset; and at times, they can be incredibly frustrating. But when customers reach out to customer service, they do so out of desperation. They turn to customer service because there's no one else to turn to. They're unable to solve their dilemma on their own, and unless customer service can rescue them, they're consigned to their current state of disappointment. When customer service people take a participatory role and act as a liaison, concierge, or consultant, they show customers that they are allies in helping the customer get the most from the product or service.

Rule 34

CHANGE HOW YOU THINK ABOUT CUSTOMER SERVICE

▶ Customers often have to wait on hold before getting the runaround from customer service, so it's no wonder they don't hesitate to switch to a competitor. In the call center, we all understand the increasing demands and decreasing resources available to meet those demands. Wait time in your call center may be unavoidable, but what is your overall customer experience? That's the ultimate question that you have to answer. If hold time is a detriment to your service experience, then it's critical that you consider alternatives. Whether it's hiring more people, training them better, implementing self-service options, reevaluating the customer onboard process for efficiencies, or even something as simple as adding a callback service, options exist, and something needs to be done.

Oracle's *2011 Customer Experience Impact Report* showed that 58 percent of customers feel their experience expectations aren't being met because a service provider is unavailable by phone or email.[1] This kind of frustration has a negative impact on keeping customers, which should change the way you think about customer service and create a sense of urgency in delivering the solutions your customers need. Being there for your customers is the key to successful service.

THE ROADMAP TO CUSTOMER SUCCESS

Connecting and engaging with customers requires rethinking the customer interaction. If the focus is on individual transactions, the ultimate experience and relationship with the customer will suffer. But a holistic approach to developing a customer—and not just hooking a buyer—is critical in the roadmap to success. A successful approach includes meeting and exceeding expectations in terms of the voice used in engaging with customers, connecting the various touch points of the customer interaction, personalizing the individual experience points to meet the needs of the customer, creating efficiencies in service operations, and rewarding customers who invest in their relationship with you.

The disconnect that creates bad service experience isn't always the fault of customer service departments, but rather a misallocation of time, attention, and resources within the organization. Going back to the drawing board and reevaluating and reworking the roadmap for engagement with customers paves the way to making the experience consistent across all customer contact channels that your organization manages.

THE CUSTOMER EXPERIENCE DISCONNECT

Much, much more can and should be done to align organizations and establish a more consistent customer service experience. Hold time is just one component of overall customer experience. Hold time is attention. It's customer care. Services today are available that can help organizations manage their hold time and even eliminate it. I'm a big fan of callback services because of the potential they have to help manage a high volume of customer service requests.

Personal, engaging customer service gives organizations an opportunity to take transparency to a whole new level in customer/company relations. Customers today crave a sense of connectedness to the people they do business with. In previous generations, it was easier for customers to connect because you did business with the owner in your local community. Globalization and the Internet have taken away that personal touch in business interactions. Too many companies hide behind a faceless corporate image.

As you become more connected and eliminate more of the communication barriers between customers and companies, it's critical that you evaluate the new technology and determine its ability to help achieve the real purpose of customer service: to make helping customers as painless as possible. Learning more about human behavior and what motivates people will make it easier for you to influence others and make a positive connection with customers during customer service interactions.

Your customers are living, breathing, feeling individuals who need care, attention, and meaning when it comes to the experience you create for them in your customer service offerings. The pace of how customer service is done has never been faster. We live in the instant age; immediate attention is now expected when it comes to customer service. This means that finding and delivering the up-to-date information customers expect has to be done quicker than ever. But for it to be done well, it needs to still be human. Real customer service is an intensely human experience between a customer with actual needs and wants and customer service professionals who are trained consultants that can utilize information, systems, and resources to help cater to the needs and wants of those served.

Rule 35

REALLY GET TO KNOW YOUR CUSTOMERS

▶ The easiest way to make sure you deliver exceptional customer service is to know exactly what your customers want. Customers love personalization. The more personal you make your delivery, the more effective you'll be with the customer interaction. The result? Loyal customers. If you were to ask individuals in your organization, "What are the top priorities for customers?" or "What are the greatest factors contributing to customer satisfaction?" could they answer these questions correctly?

Unfortunately, the disconnect between what customers really want and what people in your organization know about it is all too real. Do the customer service employees, or software developers, or accounting professionals realize the effect they have in the overall service experience of customers? When you think of the number of people who play a factor in the ability of your organization to deliver an effective service experience, it can be overwhelming. However, there's no reason to despair because, as a service professional leader, you can begin making a difference in helping the entire organization focus on service starting today. Start to talk about customer service with everybody and begin sharing the keys to getting and keeping customers happy.

SERVICE SECRETS CUSTOMERS WISH YOU KNEW
Whether your customers are telling you this through their feedback, surveys, or just in general communication, there are five simple keys to service that customers *really* wish you knew about them:

1. Customers value good service more than fast service.
2. Customers love personalization and will often pay more for it.
3. Show customers that you really care.
4. Ask what they *really* want from the customer service experience.
5. Always be ready, willing, and able to help when things go wrong.

Understanding these five points is critical to delivering effective service interactions that really create great customer experiences.

Customers Value Good Service More than Fast Service
Although fast is important, it means nothing if things are not done right. Getting service right and delivering the results that customers expect is what they really want. This has to be the foundation of your service mission. Before getting fast, make sure you've got it right.

Customers Love Personalization and Will Often Pay More for It
Nothing says "you matter" more than making service personal. It's the personal interaction that shows customers that their investment in your organization matters to you. Customers crave personalization. Find out everything you can about your customer, and then cater to their specific needs and preferences and you'll have a customer for life.

Show Customers That You Really Care
Many customers today feel that too many organizations take their business for granted. Customers will remember you if you remember them (their name). Remember to frequently give customers praise and they'll sing your praises to the world. Creating more goodwill with customers doesn't have to cost a lot. If you're stuck, find a customer frustration and solve it. Reach out to your customers. Connect with them. Get real with them. *Customer service* has a great opportunity in today's market to really make a huge difference if you take off the

chains of corporateness and strict company policies and let people connect with people.

Ask What They *Really* Want from the Customer Service Experience

A recent survey by Forrester Research showed that roughly two-thirds of organizations today were rated as delivering just an OK, poor, or very poor customer experience.[1] This fact should make organizations rethink their customer service and customer experience strategy, since the focus of their current efforts doesn't appear to be delivering the expected results.

Always Be Ready, Willing, and Able to Help When Things Go Wrong

A Harris Interactive report showed that 89 percent of customers today have actually moved to a competitor after experiencing a poor customer service interaction.[2] When customers who received a bad experience have gone online to complain and ask for resolution, nearly 80 percent said that the company never responded to their complaint. But those organizations that actually were ready, listening, and willing to work with customers were able to save more than half of their disappointed customers in the service recovery process.

Clearly more needs to be done and can be done. Too many companies are focusing on just creating processes for receiving feedback and adding customer communication channels to their toolbox of customer service, but few are taking the time to ensure that these resources are actually being used effectively. Smart companies realize that excellent customer service is a vital tool to attracting new customers and creating better loyalty from the customers you have. And that means really getting to know your customers!

TEACH YOUR PEOPLE TO ENGAGE WITH CUSTOMERS

Clarity of expectation, perhaps the most basic of employee needs in the workplace, is critical to customer service performance. Do your customer service agents really know what is expected of them? Or better yet, do they know what a successful result of their work looks like? We're talking about doing more than showing up and working a full eight hours. We often take for granted what it means to really work. But in order to get the most from your customer service people and call center agents, it takes more than simply expecting work to happen. We need to clearly express what successful work is and set the right expectations for the results from work performed.

THE HIGHER PURPOSE OF WORK

For a call center agent working in customer service, it's not enough to say that her job is to "take care of the customer" or "answer customer phone calls." Those are actions completely devoid of meaning. What is needed, instead, is direct tie-in of the job function to the overall mission or purpose for the work being done.

Exceptional customer service happens when agents work toward a higher purpose than the simple job function performed. No longer are customer questions simply answered, but a service team expertly resolves all customer concerns within one customer contact, thus ensuring that customers get the most from their product without the need for additional customer service help. Phone calls aren't just answered within 30 seconds, but customer service ensures that the customers' valuable time is rarely wasted when they contact customer service.

EMPATHY IS THE MOST IMPORTANT
CUSTOMER SERVICE SKILL

Employees know their job titles and understand general job functions. They can go through the motions and can perform the right actions. But in order to really engage the employee in a higher purpose, and get the most in terms of results, they have to see the ultimate purpose for their work. Many companies that set out to deliver better customer service today fall short of creating a customer experience that creates customer loyalty.

You won't always understand all of your customers. You might not even side with them and their service requests. But if real customer service is going to happen, you are going to have to understand their concerns and be able to make the type of decisions that will ultimately be in the best interest of each customer. True empathy on the part of the service agent can have a powerful effect on the service experience that customers get.

WHAT EMPATHY DOES FOR CUSTOMER SERVICE

Those who can truly empathize with customers reach a higher, more meaningful level of customer service that enables the impact of their actions to mean more than just a set of tasks being performed.

- ▸ You will be more likely to treat customers the way they wish you would treat them.
- ▸ You will better understand the needs of people around you.
- ▸ You will more clearly understand the perception you create in others with your words and actions.
- ▸ You will understand the unspoken parts of your communication with others.
- ▸ You will better understand the needs of your customers at work.
- ▸ You will have less trouble dealing with interpersonal conflict, wherever it occurs.
- ▸ You will be able to more accurately predict the actions and reactions of people you interact with.

▸ You will learn how to motivate the people around you.

▸ You will more effectively convince others of your point of view.

▸ You will experience the world in higher resolution, as you perceive through not only your perspective but also the perspectives of those around you.

▸ You will find it easier to deal with the negativity of others if you can better understand their motivations and fears. Lately, when I find myself personally struggling with someone, I remind myself to empathize and I immediately calm myself and accept the situation for what it is.

You will be a better leader, a better follower, and most important, a better friend. Customers may not necessarily ask for these things, but they will appreciate them. Their appreciation will keep them coming back over and over again.

CREATE A MANIFESTO
FOR SERVICE

▶ As you set out to change the face of service you and your customers experience, you'll need to enlist the help of others who care about making a difference and are willing to develop a process that will translate aspirations into actionable results. Delivering a great experience for customers inspires those who serve as they get to see the direct results of their efforts to please customers. The connection and ongoing relationship between customers and those who serve them can be a motivating factor to continually improve and innovate in the approach to service. But great experience is a condition, not an achievement.

The process of developing the service experience is more closely associated with a lifestyle than a project. Service requires constant attention, development, and insight in order to maintain excellence. No individual or organization reaches service greatness in a single step or in a single day. Even as your ability to provide quality service grows, you assume that things will follow a given course when you interact with a new customer. Each interaction is a new opportunity to show your focus.

A customer service manifesto is an essential guidebook for inspiring and motivating transformation change in organizations today. Your service manifesto is critical in order to ensure that all your people clearly understand the ideals and aspirations they should emphasize as they work to eliminate bad customer service. As you develop your manifesto for service change, identify the key conditions customers are struggling with and lay out your plan for overcoming the service issues that are all too common today.

No organization is perfect, and imperfection means service won't always live up to the standards you strive to achieve. But poor customer service is simply a stage in the overall process of developing and perfecting the customer experience. You and your people can't be content with poor service standards; they must give way to a higher standard of service in order to truly matter in today's marketplace. Your manifesto should clearly define the role of customer service in order to hold all of your people accountable for their actions on behalf of customers.

THE NEW CUSTOMER EXPERIENCE STANDARD
As you deliver exceptional service experiences, you almost immediately begin to receive positive feedback from those you serve. This vote of confidence from the people you serve should be enough to propel your ideals forward as you work to change the landscape of how service work is done. There are emerging brands today that are changing the basic foundation upon which organizations have built customer service. This new ideological approach to customer relations is changing the culture of service and leading the way to a new age of customer service.

This new system that is emerging before our eyes, the modern service experience economy, is breaking down the chains of mass production and sales built by traditional organizations. This transition of the service culture is essential in order for power to be properly rebalanced toward customers whose choices drive the value that businesses depend on to survive today. Unless this transformation takes place, customers are doomed to mediocrity that comes from the unconscious and unplanned service experiences of profit-centric corporations.

ACCOUNTABILITY, TRANSPARENCY, AND CLARITY
Accountability for service results is critical in order to transform the service experience in organizations today. Every organization should establish a leader as a customer advocate to ensure continued progress toward better service. Transparency and clarity should be the corner-

stones of the service experience. Strong frameworks for building customer relationships need to be present in every organization that cares about developing stronger bonds with customers.

Ultimately, you are accountable for the results. It's in your control whether customer relationships last or you're constantly struggling with churn. If customer needs aren't being met, it's up to you to make the changes required to ensure that they're served. If customer processes go wrong, it's your responsibility to ensure that the right people are alerted and that the support safety net can assist in the recovery before a customer is lost for good. Organizations attempting to change often claim that they will now follow the higher service standard, but few are able to prove that they actually are doing it. Put yourself in the place of the customer and ensure that customer advocates can act on the behalf of the customers you're trying to serve.

YOUR SERVICE MANIFESTO SHOULD ALWAYS BE EVOLVING

Delivering results based on your experience standards once doesn't guarantee that future interactions will yield the same results. Every team member has to look for ways to continually contribute to that overall vision of simple, easy, straightforward, and reliable service. Customers shouldn't ever feel hesitant to reach out; there should never be any question as to what they'll experience once they decide to do it. Staying on top of ongoing demands and evolving needs from customers requires constant evaluation of service design, service experience, and service results. You have to challenge the status quo. You have to stand up for what you believe in for customer service. Providing an exceptional experience can and will be part of your legacy of customer service.

TAKE CARE OF EMPLOYEES SO THEY'LL TAKE CARE OF CUSTOMERS

▶ If you want better service, make sure your employees are happy. When you take good care of your employees, they'll take good care of your customers. Customers are in charge today, and they know that they're the focus of how business is done. Customer experience is at the core of business strategy, but who's going to make it happen? Your employees!

CEOS DON'T DO CUSTOMER SERVICE

CEOs can't manage every customer interaction. VPs and managers can't take every call or respond to every email. It's just not realistic, and your business won't do well in the long term if those people are taking a big part of the inbound customer service load. Your front-line employees are the ones who really translate executive vision and mission statements into actionable, quality customer service interactions. It's the employees who deliver the return on the strategy investment.

The person on the phone taking care of the customer too often feels left out of the success the interaction will bring. Is this the right way for business to be done? It can't be. Organizations with long-term customer loyalty, increasing customer happiness, and customer engagement can't do it without taking care of their employees. Forget the statistics—take care of your employees and they'll take care of your customers. If you want to engage with your employees, you need a new approach to the employee relationship.

MAKING EMPLOYEES HAPPY IS THE FIRST STEP
TO MAKING CUSTOMERS HAPPY

Too many organizations have lost the trust of their employees. Employees aren't engaged. Employees aren't happy, or even satisfied for that matter. The result? Poor customer interactions. Unhappy employees can only fake happy customer service for so long. In time, it'll catch up with you and you'll begin to see the negative effect of bad customer service. If you can't take care of your employees, how can you expect them to take care of your customers? Unsatisfied employees can't even begin to exceed the expectations of those they service.

Imagine a starving restaurant cook or waiter being asked to serve restaurant customers. If you're starving your employees by limiting pay, learning resources, ongoing training, or advancement opportunities, you're handicapping their ability to take care of customers. Stop starving the chefs.

CREATE A POSITIVE ENVIRONMENT

Do you want to create more positive customer experiences? Start with creating a more positive employee environment. Happy and engaged employees who love what they do, have the resources to do their best, and are appreciated for the work they do are those who best engage with customers, create better customer relationships, and improve customer experiences.

A positive environment doesn't mean catered lunches or weekly after-work activities. Something as simple as the flexibility to customize a workplace or decorate a cubicle or desk is enough to help people personally connect with the work they do. Allowing employees the freedom to express themselves and personalize their approach to work works wonders in creating employee engagement and productivity and translates into positive customer outcomes.

INVEST WHERE IT MATTERS MOST

Invest in your success. Organizations that get the most from their people are those that invest the most in their success. Employee investment means continued training to help people be at their best. It means mentoring them to ensure removal of barriers that prevent them from performing at their best.

Investing in employees means encouraging education and professional development so that they are always progressing toward doing and being better than before. If your employees are successfully engaged in your mission and have the ability to take action to deliver positive results in an environment where they're valued for their contribution, it creates the capacity for greater positive interaction to take place between your people and your customers.

MAKE DATA-DRIVEN CUSTOMER DECISIONS AND TAKE PEOPLE-CENTRIC ACTION

We are living in an era of constant customer engagement. Customer engagement is more complex today than ever before, and yet, customer expectations for what they should get from companies have never been higher. Companies need to engage customers during the pre-sales, through the purchase process, and in post-purchase customer service and product support.

There is a constant need to engage with customers consistently throughout the entire customer life cycle in order to keep the customers you've acquired. The old "push" method of engaging customers no longer works effectively. Today, customers expect to create their own engagement model with companies, based on their own needs and wants. Social media and smartphones have changed the *customer engagement* paradigm. Customers are empowered with digital information and the ability to share negative or positive views about companies via social media.

ENGAGING CUSTOMERS THROUGH MULTIPLE CHANNELS

Traditional and social channels have combined to create multichannel engagement. Customers want to engage 24/7/365 and ensure their choice of channel doesn't disadvantage them, based on their preferences. If you want mobile shopping, then you expect your favorite Main Street store to also offer its products via mobile. If you want to view handbags in-store and then purchase via your mobile, the retailer should cater to this.

Digital shopping and the growth of noncash payments deliver a rich seam of customer data insights. Many companies are only just starting to learn to use data-driven insight in an appropriate way. This will lead to a new customer profitability model. Engaging customers via the right channel, with the right message, and at the right time, requires operational agility to ensure measurably profitable outcomes. The new rules of customer engagement require that companies go beyond customer-centricity and focus on human-centricity. What does this jargon mean? In simple layman terms, it means that your customers are human and they engage with humans in your company. This enables human dialogue. *Pushing* can be viewed as a company monologue, which turns customers off and may result in a customer diatribe in social media.

IDENTIFYING PROFITABLE CUSTOMER INSIGHTS

Not all customers are equally profitable. Some customers do not have the potential to become your most profitable customers. Companies are challenged to spend their budgets more effectively, while their market and their customers are becoming more diverse and sophisticated. The answer is to develop personalized or segmented communications that can be behaviorally targeted to customers. Identifying customer life cycle stages can help to focus the delivery of key insights:

- *Acquisition*: Enhance targeting to reduce acquisition costs and increase likely lifetime value.
- *Activation*: Ensure that acquisition leads to effective early engagement.
- *Engagement*: Understand customer preferences and interests.
- *Satisfaction*: Ensure service effectiveness and efficiency.
- *Loyalty*: Build deep customer relationships and focus acquisition activity.
- *Advocacy*: Reduce marketing costs through using advocates to engage prospects and customers.

Life cycle velocity will vary by customer and may not be sequential. Customers can skip one or multiple stages of the cycle at any point. If they are in a loyalty program and become dissatisfied, then they can skip forward straight to disengage. Customers may leave your brand forever when they disengage. Keep in mind that the new rules of customer engagement are data-driven, yet human-centric.

Rule 40

CUSTOMER EXPERIENCE IS MORE IMPORTANT THAN ADVERTISING

▶ A report by Satmetrix showed that on average, less than 5 percent of customers trust advertising the most as their source of service information.[1] Yet advertisers spend hundreds of billions of dollars each year to sell to their customers. The billion-dollar-a-year advertising club is made up of famous brands such as Procter & Gamble, General Motors, Verizon, Comcast, AT&T, JPMorgan Chase, Ford, American Express, Disney, Walmart, and McDonald's.

You might argue that these organizations are also massively profitable. True. But do you have a billion dollars to spend in advertising each year?

You can't discount the usefulness of advertising, as organizations still require it to build awareness, develop a brand, and launch new products and services. But with fewer and fewer customers who trust advertising as the source of information about products and services, you have to turn to a more profitable source of reaching customers. Experience is a viable means for creating and keeping customers today.

SPREADING THE WORD

Word of mouth carries a big, heavy stick when it comes to the reputation of your products and services. There are strong trends showing that consumers are looking for sources beyond traditional advertising when they make purchasing decisions. Half of consumers, in a study done by Satmetrix, cited recommendations from personal connections as the most trustworthy source of information.[2] Facebook, Twitter, Yelp, and other social media and reviews sites help to amplify the voice of the customer. YouTube product reviews, service experience blog reviews, and frustrations vented on social media sites are no longer private, but open to everybody to consider and use when making their next purchase.

The Internet has given incredible power to people to voice their experience about a product or service and the interaction they've had with an organization. A single bad customer service experience posted online can spiral out of control, tarnishing the image of an organization that has taken years to build. The infamous Comcast "phone call from hell" isn't limited to just Comcast; any organization with an agent having a bad day is vulnerable to a poor service experience. But when the customer on the other end is an editor for a major online magazine, as happened with Comcast, a bad service experience can quickly turn into a customer service nightmare. Just participating in social media also doesn't mean you're really engaging with customers. Given the power of social communication today, it's critical that you focus on investing in customer service.

WHY CUSTOMER EXPERIENCE MATTERS

Your reputation for great customer service can create the incentive for customers to give you a try. Some of your most loyal customers will be those who have seen you show that your customers really matter to you. And they will often describe their positive customer experience in social media. Good experience grabs potential new customers, and your great customer service can be a vehicle for generating sales and helping the bottom line. The bottom line is keeping those customers once they've given your company a shot.

When bad experiences happen, you have an opportunity to make things right. Make sure you are listening to your customers, old and new, especially when they complain about something. When customers are left without options to solve their problems, they take to their social networks to vent. These customers will do all they can to warn others of the terrible experience of working with your organization.

The Internet has amplified the ability for news to travel instantly, especially bad news. Therefore, many customer service management software providers focus on developing more effective tools to help you stay on top of managing your customer experience and ensuring that your customers are getting good customer service from your staff, all of the time. Consider investing in a better customer service experience.

MAKE CONSISTENCY A CRITICAL CUSTOMER METRIC

▶ Customer experience and customer service are not the same thing, although customer service is certainly a big part of a customer's experience. Customer experience is a whole lot more than customer service: it's the culmination of all facets of customer service and how your customers experience them.

In dealing with your organization, your customers will be experiencing various aspects of your customer service actions, such as how they are spoken to on the phone, the appearance and cleanliness of your building and facilities, the personality and appearance of your staff, the effectiveness and efficiency of the service you provide, or the usability of the product they purchase. These are just a few aspects of customer service; there are many more. Any of them can affect the customer's experience. Imagine being at your local restaurant where the service was outstanding and the food was excellent, but the kitchen noises were way too loud and the hostess was quite rude. Regardless of how great the customer service and the food were, your overall customer experience would be considered very poor.

CUSTOMER EXPERIENCE IS A STRATEGY

The "strategy" of customer experience involves every single customer service touch point in your business, with everything and everyone working together as a whole to make your customer's experience a positive one. A really good customer experience is a genuine one, sincere and heartfelt—but above all, it must be consistent. This doesn't just happen by itself; it involves consistent and extensive training in order to understand the importance of a client's experience, to plan your customer experience strategy, and to ensure that each and every staff member is aware that a top-quality customer experience is your number one priority.

Through training, you should endeavor to create positive and lasting improvements to your customer service in your organization, which will create fantastic customer experiences and drive revenue growth. The whole idea is to provide such exceptional customer service in all areas of your organization that the total customer experience will stay in your customer's mind for a long time to come.

YOU DON'T FORGET AMAZING CUSTOMER SERVICE

During a recent stay at a famous local resort, I was taken aback at the top-notch customer service and commitment to customer experience that I saw from all staff members who interacted with me. In the one week I stayed in this fabulous establishment, I had no negative experiences, and never once felt like the service was lacking in any way. It was a terrific experience. Every staff interaction throughout the week was consistent and pleasant. From the gift shop attendant, the concierge, housekeepers, restaurant, bar, and particularly the staff at the front desk—they all did everything in their power to ensure that my stay was as pleasant as could be.

I could clearly see that the entire organization was involved in ongoing and up-to-date customer service training. I was delighted to receive a friendly "hello" from housemaids working in the hotel, and even the gardeners always had something pleasant to say. When everyone says "Good morning!" or "Good evening!" with such wonderful smiles, it really does brighten up your day. This hotel understands the true value of providing an excellent customer experience, and they certainly do it right. It's all about consistency; there was never a lapse in service—from anyone.

CUSTOMER EXPERIENCE STRATEGY
MUST BE CONSISTENT

In a hotel, consistency in great customer service to all customers is vital. People often spend many days, sometimes weeks, in hotels—either on business or for pleasure—and it's so important that there is no inconsistency in the service provided. But consistent service experience is vital to all types of organizations. Whether you rely on repeat business or mostly see customers just once, experience is how you sustain your business.

Whether experiences that matter are created and all team members are performing at the right level to deliver exceptional service varies among different organizations. Most places will have one or maybe a few individuals who understand what it takes to provide great service. You see this as customers begin to ask for certain people by name any time they deal with the organization. But service excellence and creating a lasting legacy for service means ensuring that all members of the organization—not just a few individuals—share the same passion for service. Consistency should be the guiding principle.

MAKE SURE YOUR PEOPLE TAKE CARE OF THEMSELVES

▶ The words *happiness* and *call center* seem contradictory when used in the same sentence. But we do depend on happiness in the workplace to provide excellent customer service. And nowhere is this more important than in call centers where people are constantly dealing with anger, frustration, and stress. It stands to reason that the key to excellent customer service in organizations that continually outperform their competitors is, in fact, the happiness of the service agents. We've created a list of sensible ideas to help you and your people become happier—ideas that are backed by science.

EXERCISE

Did you know that exercise has proven to be an effective way to overcome depression? Exercise has a profound effect on our well-being and ultimately our level of happiness. In the book titled *The Happiness Advantage* (Crown Business 2010), Shawn Achor discusses a study in which people suffering from depression were divided into three groups: one group was treated with medication, another with exercise, and the third received a combination of the two. The results of the study were surprising because all three groups noticed similar improvements in their level of happiness. However, follow-up assessments were entirely different. After six months, the individuals were tested again, and only the group that had simply exercised retained their improved levels of happiness.

Customer service can be a grueling job. Hours and hours of constant people interaction can be draining. Exercise not only improves our health but also builds up the endurance we need to keep up with the physical demands of customer service work.

GO TO SLEEP

When you get adequate sleep, you'll be much less sensitive to negative feelings and emotions. While we sleep our bodies begin to recover and repair themselves from our busy day. Getting enough quality sleep enables us to focus and be productive during the day. And it affects our happiness. We need rest; when we don't get it, we suffer. We're not as sharp in our skills and talents. We're prone to be angry. We're more sensitive to what others do and say. Exceptional service requires doing our best in each service interaction, every single day. People in customer service have to deal with challenging circumstances and upset customers. When we're not mentally at our best, the service experience clearly suffers.

SPEND QUALITY TIME WITH FRIENDS AND FAMILY

It's often said that on the deathbed, no one ever says, "I wish I had spent more time at work." Research proves that you can become happier right now just by making contact with those you love and who love you in return. Even for the shy or introverted, social time is extremely valuable and necessary for improving happiness. Generally, time well spent with family and friends makes a huge difference in how happy we feel.

GET SOME FRESH AIR

Spending time outside in the fresh air is sure to improve your happiness. On a nice day, plan to spend time outside: This will boost your mood, improve your memory, and broaden your thinking. Most of us can spare 20 minutes out of our busy schedules—it could mean spending your lunch hour in the park.

MAKE A DIFFERENCE TO OTHERS

This one is so simple, yet we forget about it all too often. If we want to be happy ourselves, all we have to do is make someone else happy. When we help someone else, we enrich our own lives so much. You only need to dedicate a couple of hours a week and this will change your life. The simple act of doing a kindness for another human being increases our well-being more than any other known exercise.

SMILE

Did you know that smiling can alleviate pain? Even if you don't feel like smiling, just do it anyway. Smile at people as you pass them by—you may make a huge difference to someone else's day. After a while, your smile won't feel forced—you will actually feel better yourself. Then you need to back up that smile with some positive thoughts. Every person has something to be grateful for; thinking about your blessings should bring a smile to your face. Besides making us feel happier, smiling also helps us see life through a different lens—one where we can see better and more clearly.

MEDITATE

Meditation is great for improving clarity, focus, attention, and inner peace, but it's also wonderful as a rewiring process for happiness. The idea of meditation is to clear your mind, allowing you to be in a state of calmness. It's believed to be one of the most effective ways of creating a happier life.

In the moments after meditating, we experience wonderful feelings of contentment and calm, in addition to empathy and heightened awareness. We now know that meditation is also capable of permanently rewiring the brain to increase happiness levels, changing the way we think and feel.

BE GRATEFUL

Practicing gratitude will increase your satisfaction with life, in addition to making you feel much happier. This sounds simplistic, and in a way, it is. If you practice gratitude through regular journaling, or share three great things about your day with a family member or friend, or just feel grateful when someone does something nice for you, your happiness level will increase. As you're drifting off to sleep, say (or whisper) all the things you're grateful for. It's a lovely way to go to sleep, and you'll invariably wake up feeling happy in the morning. You can write letters of gratitude, and there is evidence that just writing the words will increase your satisfaction with life and boost your happiness.

AS YOU CAN SEE, happiness doesn't cost money. You don't need a luxurious car or a new job, and you don't need others to provide happiness for you. You are in control of your own happiness, and you do have the power to make it happen. Remember that you always have a choice. If there is something about your life that you don't like, or absolutely hate, then change it. You are the only one who can do it, because you're in control of your own happiness.

DISPEL CUSTOMERS' FEAR OF CUSTOMER SERVICE

▶ Fear is often caused by the conviction that someone or something is dangerous, but in the case of contacting customer support, it is altogether different. The dread of contacting service support is due to the fact that most people strongly believe it's not going to work out. Somehow, we subconsciously assume that the customer service representative will not be able to understand our problem and provide a relevant solution to it.

IDENTIFYING REASONS FOR CUSTOMER FEARS

All this fear and subliminal negation is attributable to the terrible experiences we may have had in the past in this regard. Some of the main reasons for dreading contact with customer service include the following:

▸ People often complain that customer support service providers sound frustrated and tend to give curt or rude replies, rather than being pleasant and helpful.
▸ Telecom services can be poor and disconnections are frequent. It's aggravating to explain your problem in detail to one rep, then suddenly hear a disconnection tone, and have to call back to repeat the process from the beginning.
▸ Callers often must spend endless minutes on hold. This can be really exasperating for a person who is asking for help with an immediate problem.
▸ Many times, calls get disconnected after the customer has been on hold for several minutes.

▸ Because of inadequate training, callers are often transferred from one customer support service representative to another because none of them seem to know how to solve the particular issue at hand.

HELPING CUSTOMERS OVERCOME THEIR FEAR

These fears generally get into customers' heads because previous companies have offered appalling customer support experiences. Such companies work in a sales-first fashion and don't pay much heed to the concept and practice of customer support. You can avoid this if you focus all your hard work on development of well-informed customer support personnel.

Stellar customer service helps to overcome such awful customer service experiences as those described above. You can create a better reputation with regard to customer support service by designing an integrated platform that lets customer support representatives understand the customer's needs and problems comprehensively and attend to requests suitably.

Perhaps it's time to adopt some new tools and provide more multichannel support options so that customers don't need to connect through traditional support methods. They can use live chat, email, and self-service tools. Companies like WalkMe are available to allow businesses to adopt self-service channels into their customer service department. They guide the users through their smaller-issue task until they have completed the task. There's no need for them to fear calling the contact center when they have managed to fix the issue on their own.

Management personnel in all companies, big and small, need to understand that it's not only sales that are important. Having a good customer support team helps a company develop a long-term relationship with its customer base. Providing timely after-sales services helps build goodwill. Hence, customer satisfaction should be the prime concern, not profit maximization alone. Give them the tools they need to survive so that they don't scare customers away.

LEARN HOW TO EARN YOUR CUSTOMER'S LOYALTY

The most successful organizations are those that realize the true value of nurturing lasting relationships with customers. In today's competitive environment, holding on to your existing customers can be the key to survival. In short, customer loyalty matters, and creating customer loyalty will need to be a key component of your business success strategy.

Many companies failed to do this before the recession, focusing on shorter-term quick wins that left them with a disloyal and unappealing customer base. In order to maximize sales from existing customers, a company must focus on three principles:

1. *Identify* loyal customers.
2. *Deliver* above-and-beyond customer service.
3. *Establish* an upsell/cross-sell strategy that rewards loyalty and advocacy.

Building customer loyalty doesn't happen naturally. It takes specific work and strategy. Here are some practical customer loyalty concepts to consider as you build your most loyal customer base.

IDENTIFY YOUR POTENTIAL LOYAL CUSTOMERS

Before you can increase your revenue per customer, you need to understand which of your customers offer you the best opportunities for maximum growth. Identifying your most loyal customers is a solid starting point, as they are likely to be open to the idea of spending more if you can offer them something of interest. A simple analysis of your customers will not only help maximize the revenue they bring, but it can also help attract new customers with a similar profile.

Next, you need to analyze their buying behavior. Find out when and what they buy, as well as their interests and preferences. Create profile groups to identify different groups of loyal customers: Do some groups hold more potential than others or require a different approach to customer management? The more you segment your customer base, the more focused you will be and the greater the potential for increasing loyalty and spending.

DELIVER CUSTOMER SERVICE BEYOND
WHAT CUSTOMERS EXPECT

Once you've identified your loyal customers, you need to ensure they're as happy as possible. This will maximize the likelihood of retaining them and make them open to spending more with you. Customer satisfaction is essential to building long-term, profitable relationships. To achieve this, a business first needs to understand what its customers think of it. Invite them to give feedback so you can identify what you could be doing better and, just as important, what you are doing well already. It's not enough to just meet the needs of customers. That's setting the bar too low and could result in underwhelming the customers, leaving them open to being tempted by competitors who could offer more of what customers want.[1]

My friend Bill Quiseng, resort manager at the Marriott Ko Olina Beach Club in Oahu, Hawaii, always reminds me of the need to strive for something beyond meeting needs. He says, "Nobody raves about average; think relationships or go broke." To achieve the level of connection with customers that keeps them loyal, there needs to be a little more in the service experience, an unexpected pleasantry for the customer in order to go beyond just simple satisfaction.

ENGAGE CUSTOMERS TO REWARD
LOYALTY AND ADVOCACY

Communicating with your customers also provides you with the opportunity to confirm whether their expectations have been met, make them aware of other products they may be interested in, and express appreciation for their business. With an increasing number of retailers now active online, communication with customers has never been more important. We are human after all, and having that personal connection with those from whom we buy will encourage repeat orders and loyalty.

Providing excellent customer service can not only increase customers' spending but also make customers fiercely loyal advocates of your brand. Customer advocacy (which stems from customer satisfaction and loyalty) is a critical stepping-stone on the path to deliver a quantifiable return on your business investment. Understanding this, and then developing training, processes, and procedures that support your customer-facing staff, is essential for almost every business looking to improve customer loyalty.

Finally, make sure you reward customer loyalty, whether it's offering discounts, a freebie, loyalty points, or preferential service. This strategy can be more effective than traditional customer loyalty marketing or just including discussions about customer loyalty in company training. Loyalty matters, and customer loyalty should be rewarded as well as viewed as a potential source of additional revenue that affects your bottom line.

Rule 45

FORGET MISSION STATEMENTS; CREATE ACTION STATEMENTS

Mission statements don't inspire outstanding customer service; action statements are the motivators needed to get your people doing great things. The problem with mission statements is they aren't real. Mission statement language often lacks the human touch. It's usually corporate jargon–filled, wordy, and stale. Traditional mission statements don't translate into something with purpose, something that inspires action within your organization and in those charged with delivering excellent customer service.

If you asked most of your employees to recite the company mission statement, how do you think they would respond? If you guessed *silence*, you're probably right. The problem is that mission statements are often so vague that most employees don't know what they're really supposed to do. They don't see how to translate them into action.

MOST EMPLOYEES IGNORE MISSION STATEMENTS

One of the challenges of leading organizations in a customer-focused approach is that you, at the top, generally will be the most inspired, most enthusiastic, most motivated individual with the passion for the customer. Gobbledy-gook mission statements are often forgotten by, misremembered, or flatly ignored by frontline employees. Rarely will you find a rank-and-file team member who is just as passionate about the cause. There may be some, but they are few and far between. That's just the reality of doing business.

MISSION STATEMENTS ARE OFTEN
OVERSTUFFED WITH KEYWORDS

If mission statements today were evaluated by Google's search algorithm, most companies would be penalized like a shady SEO company trying to stuff in every possible keyword and term related to doing business. Mission statements today often more closely resemble word clouds of business terms than an actual vision for what matters to the business and how its people are going to act to achieve it. Instead of trying to jam-pack every possible aspiration into your corporate mission statement that no one will remember except you, focus instead on an action statement that can be the core of everything you do.

HOW TO WRITE A GREAT MISSION STATEMENT

Forget the traditional sample mission statements. Free mission statements that you find online won't cut it.

Make It an Action Statement

The best mission statement is an action statement.

- Action statements are *lean*.
- Action statements are *transparent*.
- Action statements are focused on *human action*.
- Action statements don't describe what you hope to be doing, but *what you pledge to your customers you will actually do*.

Instead of having "a mission to dramatically initiate performance-based opportunities as well as to proactively leverage existing quality leadership skills to meet our customer's needs," focus on something more simple, more real, and more action-oriented.

Keep It Short

In order for your action statement to make an impact that leads to lasting change, it has to be focused enough that every person in the organization can recite it with ease. The fewer words used, the greater the effect the action statement will have within your organization.

Think simple. Think action.

> Suggestion: *Verb or noun > target > outcome or result. But feel free to make up your own.*

▸ *"Provide the best customer service possible."* – Zappos
▸ *"SSL Certificate Management Done Right and Made Easy."* – DigiCert
▸ *"Save money. Live better."* – Walmart
▸ *"Inspire and nurture the human spirit—one person, one cup and one neighborhood at a time."* – Starbucks
▸ *"Whole Foods, Whole People, Whole Planet."* – Whole Foods

Every member of the organization must know the action statement, understand it, and act on it. Knowing how an action statement fits into the day-to-day role of each individual employee is the most critical element for transformative change within an organization. If you want an entire organization united and committed to delivering exceptional customer experiences, its members have to see their role as a critical point that can make or break the customer experience. Don't ever assume people know it. Quiz them. If employees can't repeat it and identify their contribution to the action statement, it's not their fault; it's yours.

As you do this, you will see the real, positive effect these statements can have in uniting and aligning people around the customer service mission, which positively affects customer loyalty and the bottom line. Once you've reached this level of understanding and commitment to your action statement, it then must become the basis for decisions made by the organization and how the actions of the group are measured for effectiveness.

GET THE CEO INTERACTING WITH CUSTOMERS

▶ We have been in the business of training organizations, companies, and individuals on customer service for over 15 years in the Asian and European markets. People always ask us for that one secret key to excellence in customer service. They expect us to provide an elaborate diagram of some complex algorithm or provide a long and lengthy conversation about culture and processes. But when you're talking customer excellence, it's entirely the opposite. And when we do give the answer, many of our clients are really taken aback.

HOW OFTEN DOES THE CEO INTERACT WITH CUSTOMERS?

The basic secret to real excellence in customer service lies in one simple question: How often does the CEO talk to the company's customers? Yes, this is the only question we believe will answer all the other questions and is the best barometer for the success of the customer life cycle management of any organization striving for customer service excellence. The CEO is the ultimate engine driver and harbinger for the basic unit of customer satisfaction—the smile. The smile resonates when the customers realize that it comes from all spheres of the organization, especially the CEO. That's a critical component to achieving customer service excellence.

Think about it. The model is clear. People at the bottom, whom we consider as foot soldiers, have to take care of the customers. That is their job and that is what they are getting paid to do. Middle management is responsible for the monitoring and evaluation of the tasks, transactions, and even the overall cradle-to-grave customer expectation model. Excellence in customer service training is a must. Without that constant review, customer excellence isn't possible.

Management is a service function. The role of senior management isn't necessarily to be the smartest people in the organization, but they certainly should be the wisest at determining which ideas are best for the organization and how to tailor those ideas to fit the strategic vision of long-term success in acquiring and retaining the most precious commodity of the organization: its customers.

Effective CEOs and senior managers must understand that service excellence is more than just an aspiration. They are the standard-bearers, and the organization will ultimately follow that standard as it marches forward. Leading an organization today effectively must be done through crystal clear vision and goals that every member of the organization trusts and understands.

HOW MUCH TIME DOES MANAGEMENT SPEND ON CUSTOMER-FOCUSED ACTIVITIES?

The ultimate ability to deliver customer excellence comes down to the mindset and execution of the leaders at the top. Customer service excellence requires buy-in at the top. How many hours in a day does he spend listening to the customers? How many visits does she have lined up in the months ahead? How many customers are waiting to meet the chief operating officer?

Let me shed some interesting light on this. If you were asked to define excellence in customer service, what would you say? In a recent training session with a large international pharmaceutical company, the concern was that the input from the customers was not being heard. Customers were giving feedback about package, pricing, and service changes. When the CEO was asked how many times he has heard it directly from the business customers, his reply was silence. You don't need people to tell you how bad the business is. You can get it from going directly to the heart of the issue—the voice of the customer.

WHAT FACTORS IMPROVE
CUSTOMER SATISFACTION?

In our research on customer satisfaction, the better the CEO is in dealing with, handling, and fostering long-term growth with the customer, the better the long-term success in terms of revenues, opportunities, and customer excellence ratings. People watch and see. If the CEO is busy meeting and greeting the customers, then management realizes the importance of the customer and where the company is going. In fact, we recommend the CEO take along other people from the organization to meet the customers. It's a wake-up call for many people worldwide.

Ensure that the CEO is busy migrating his workload into the customer domain. Without this, all the culture processes and procedures do not work. If you want to be known as a leader in customer excellence, it's not just the people at the front that need training; it requires the combined effort from everyone in the organization. And that includes the person at the top!

LEARN TO OBSESS
OVER CUSTOMERS

In the early 1900s, manufacturing controlled markets and the attention of businesses. During the late 1900s and early 2000s information was power, and organizations that could harness its power were able to yield exceptional results. Lately, we've seen a transformation in the way businesses approach their strategic initiatives. We're slowly experiencing a shift in the balance of power in consumer transactions today. Supply chains and mass manufacturing, combined with the power of big data and information service, have actually tilted the power back in favor of customers, and organizations are learning to obsess over customers.

The organizations that have adapted the quickest to these new standards of doing business are capitalizing on this shift and changing the nature of how business is done. Today, engagement is everything. Organizations that emphasize customer obsession are seeing positive results and have learned to change their approach when they consider what makes up great customer service. Obsession over building service teams, delivering the right kind of service, creating the service environment, setting the right tone for service, and having laser-like focus on service results sets them apart from those struggling to remain relevant to customers.

OBSESS OVER THE SERVICE TEAM

It takes time to build up the perfect team to get service right. Not everyone has what it takes and others may not even know that they're made for customer service. Obsess over whom you choose to enlist in your efforts. Obsess over what the best fit is for each person you choose. Work to create the best possible team to deliver the best possible customer service.

OBSESS OVER THE RIGHT KIND OF SERVICE

Make sure you have confidence in the entire customer service team. Empower the frontline services team by allowing them to respond innovatively/proactively no matter what the situation because they can be trusted to do the job well. This acts like a catalyst that influences credibility and ultimately has a direct impact on overall customer service results.

OBSESS OVER THE SERVICE ENVIRONMENT

Customer service needs to be an inviting, positive, and welcoming environment. The customers need a positive atmosphere and engagement on a personal level. They expect enthusiasm, and they deserve more than just politeness, smiles, or robotic routines like, "How may I be of assistance to you today?" Customers need to feel that you are friendly, enthusiastic, and helpful, and that your service will reliably deliver timely solutions to any problem. However, you should aim to deliver even more—something above and beyond any other competitor's style of service.

OBSESS OVER THE SERVICE TONE

Win your customers through the words you choose to say, how you say them, and the meaning behind the message. Treating other people as you would expect to be treated yourself is a key component of effective customer service. The customer's mood needs to be uplifted by using the right winning words, like "We can definitely take care of this problem," or "Consider your problem solved," and so on.

OBSESS OVER THE SERVICE RESULT

Customer barriers need to be dispersed, broken, and eliminated from the service experience. The service has to be rapidly responsive to be able to quickly engage with the customers and develop a relationship with them but still get the communication absolutely right the first time round. Whatever we do that is special for that individual customer does not mean that every other customer will expect or even want exactly the same service.

You'll rarely get a chance to go back and redo your initial customer impression. Every customer interaction, every service touch point, may be the only time you'll get to show your customers your actual focus. Get it right and you can create a customer for life. Get it wrong and you probably won't see that customer again. Great customer service can generate powerful momentum for your organization. Exceptional customer experiences connect your customers with your brand in a way that is more than just about doing business; it's about changing life. Begin an attitude check today and go out and use your exceptional customer service attitude to win the customer.

Rule 48

DEFINE CUSTOMER FOCUS
FOR YOUR COMPANY

▶ Deciding to do something about the service you deliver is the easy part. Actually making effective things happen for your customers is the struggle. It's easy to meet with your people and make service experience a core value for your organization, but transforming the thoughts, feelings, and actions of every individual involved in the experience, even when the only person is you, can be difficult. The two words *customer* and *service* may seem simple enough to understand, but translating them into specific processes and frameworks for delivering results only comes after great effort and hard work.

Although we generally aspire to provide great service, the type of results that really matter to customers don't often come naturally. Actionable, value-specific results aren't just a byproduct of having the right environment in the office, or the fact that you have service people on hand to talk to customers. These factors play a part in achieving outstanding customer service, but they don't actually make it happen. Customer service quality is a manifestation of your customer care and the degree of your customer focus. The lengths to which you go to serve your customers show the true essence of its existence of your organization.

Service is a reflection of your values, philosophy, ethics, beliefs, attitudes, and behaviors. What you ultimately do or don't do for your customers will impact the end results for your organization. Building on the foundation of serving customers leads to greater satisfaction and increased customer retention, and paves the way for customer loyalty and advocacy. Believe in the power that customer service has for transforming the nature of your business relationships. Believe in the connection between customer loyalty and new opportunities for growth. Believe that customer focus is not only a feel-good business endeavor, but also a requirement for long-term business success.

THE RIGHT REASONS

Effective customer service happens when you do it for the right reasons. Real customer service is more than answering phones and returning emails. It's more than responding to questions and doing things for customers. Customer service is about dispelling concerns about products and services. It's about connecting people with products and services that improve work and life. Working in customer service is about helping people take that next step and move forward, making things better. Customer service is about being supportive when frustration starts to set in and before despair causes customers to give up. When you really serve customers, you instill hope, build lasting relationships, and bring smiles to the faces of those you touch. Answering phones and replying to emails are just the mechanics of customer service; the people and experiences you touch are the reward.

THE RIGHT ATTITUDE

The attitude you embrace as you set out to serve sets the tone for what will happen with your customers. The experience you deliver will largely depend on the choices and decisions you make. The right answers to customer questions delivered with the wrong tone or attitude can defeat the customer interaction. Poor attitude consistently eats away at the relationship you're building with customers until you reach the point where no price, features, or services offered will keep the customer working with you.

Attitude can make all the difference when it comes to truly delivering exceptional results. Often, customer interactions and individual customer concerns come about from lapses in the normal course of action, requiring service recovery to step in and set things right. Especially in circumstances where the natural workflow of the customer has been disrupted, there's no second chance to get it back on track. Having a poor attitude and lack of understanding and empathy when the customer is already frustrated can set the experience on a course of no return.

THE RIGHT ACTIONS

New software systems with all the bells and whistles don't create great service experiences. Adding more and more options to your phone menu to route customers to the most appropriate agent doesn't guarantee that the most appropriate results will take place. Waiting 20-plus minutes on the phone while a recording tells you that your call is very important certainly doesn't make you feel like it is. Neither do you feel extra special when you email a quick question, only to immediately receive an automated response telling you to expect to wait 24 to 48 hours for a reply.

Real customer service needs to be free of the barriers that are too often set up in the contact center today. Too many organizations have gone out of their way to do everything possible to actually hold off customers and make sure they actually *don't* try to contact customer service. Have you ever been asked to register on a portal before being able to email customer service? Have you ever tried to find a service phone number only to have it buried or not even listed on a website? If so, you're not alone. But just because it's been done to you doesn't mean it's right. You're actually contributing to customer *dis*-service.

In order for exceptional results to come about from service interactions, the layers insulating the organization from its customers need to be peeled away. This doesn't mean that there shouldn't be a place for technology. Quite the contrary. Technological solutions today actually can enhance the customer experience and your ability to deliver real service.

THE RIGHT RESULTS

The lean startup movement can certainly be used as a model for the lean contact center. As you work toward creating unity in service vision and consistency in service results, you'll begin to reap the benefits that naturally come from true customer focus. Today, we're seeing the way service is done transform from the traditional, strict, and overly formal business processes to transparent and personal approaches. In order to get the most from the service culture, it's key that the right processes be put in place so that you can measure the effect of your service actions and ensure that you're delivering the results that your customers want.

Rule 49

LET DATA DRIVE MORE INFORMED SERVICE

▶ The main problem for most organizations that set out to deliver exceptional service isn't just acting on their desires for better service, but being able to gauge the effectiveness of the service delivered. Knowing how to measure and translate the data acquired from customer service is vital in being able to continually improve the service delivery and determine that the service experience is yielding the right results. No matter what your company does or the industry you're in, data provide valuable insight and can open the door to identifying the most effective differentiators you can use to set yourself apart from the numerous other options customers have today. Focusing on the value of customer analytics will allow you to measure the right actions and act on the insights gained.

Four key types of data will provide you with the valuable information you need:

1. *Predictive* customer data should give you insight into trends and expected results based on current market and service conditions.
2. *Prescriptive* data outline the optimal service experience and what you should strive to accomplish in your service results.
3. *Descriptive* data determine what is currently happening in your organization or what has happened in previous service engagements.
4. *Diagnostic* data determine why specific service results happened and what key factors contributed to the ultimate result.

Balancing the information to be gained from these various data types can be tricky, but it can be done as you focus on three primary ways that the data should impact the way you manage service.

DATA SHOULD BREAK DOWN BARRIERS

Collecting data from every customer interaction point is essential in order to ensure that customers receive consistent service throughout their various interactions with your organization. Not all contact channels are the same. Analyze what happens in each type and measure them against typical industry trends to ensure that you're excelling over benchmark results. As organizations mature and service teams grow, various contact channels become independent groups and the tendency for disconnect between the various service deliveries grow. Organizing available service data should give greater insight into the current conditions of service and enable a 360-degree view of the customer.

DATA SHOULD IDENTIFY WHAT IS IMPORTANT

Traditional service metrics often drive unintended results. For example, call center metrics, such as average handle time or average length of service contact, often encourage agents to speed through customer interactions or escalate more calls to upper-level agents in order to get to the next service call. Actions like this impact the metrics in a positive way but ruin the ultimate service result.

Customer-focused organizations are looking beyond the traditional data metrics and diving deeper to get greater insights into what truly matters to customers. Emphasize the metrics that correlate with positive customer experiences, like promptness in answering, speed of response, first-call resolution, net promoter score, and experience ratings.

DATA SHOULD BE USED TO DRIVE ACTION

Collecting data is often the easy part. Internalizing the information and creating actionable results that translate to what's happening on the front lines often proves much more difficult to actually do. Information is static. Data simply provide insight on services rendered. Learning from and incorporating the data is where the true value of data is found. Making informed decisions based on data is what separates the exceptional service organizations from those that simply offer a service. Acting on the insights gained from data is how differentiation takes place.

As you look at customer choices and preferences, you can customize the service experience in order to deliver maximum impact to customers. Your organization will see great results.

Rule 50

FOCUS ON THE VALUE OF GREAT SERVICE EXPERIENCE

▶ The sad state of customer service today is evident in the fact that too many organizations see customer service as a cost center. Too often, customer service is seen as sunk cost to a business, something that has to be done but that delivers little value to the bottom line. The truth is that customer service is not a neutral factor in your business. It either makes you money or costs you money.

THE VALUE OF GREAT SERVICE

Research published by Forrester answers the question of the financial payoff to organizations that invest in customer service and experience. The authors of the report concluded, "Customer service experiences either generate or diminish company revenue."[1] They go on to say, "Customer service has a *profound effect* on a corporation's bottom line."[2] Organizations that make service a competitive advantage retain their customers longer, leading to greater profits to the organization. In a *Harvard Business Review* report, researchers determined that companies that boosted their customer retention by as little as 5 percent saw increases of 25 percent to 95 percent in overall profit.[3] In the new economy in which we operate, traditional strategies of cost cutting and low-skill labor reliance are quickly proving ineffective at retaining a sufficient percentage of customers to deliver the value required from the investment made to acquire customers in the first place.

Organizations today must undergo a strategic shift in mentality and priorities as they work to streamline the processes they have in place to serve today's customers. We're not talking about carving out massive budgets for service groups, but greater strategic attention is required in the allocation of resources within the organization to deliver the effective experience results that will retain customers over the long run. Some of this realignment of resources includes shifting emphasis to new service technologies like proactive customer live chat, customer consulting through co-browsing, self-service portals and customer communities, and multichannel communications for customer service.

POOR EXPERIENCES HURT RETENTION, LEADING TO LOWER PROFITS

Oftentimes, customers who stop doing business with a company do so because of *poor or indifferent customer service and an inability for an organization to deliver what is meaningful for the customer.* A 2012 study by Verint Systems showed that customers quickly become dissatisfied with poor service experience, and in the absence of service, choose price as the differentiator between competitors.[4] Further results from the study pointed out that customers who feel that their service provider delivers a more complete service solution than its competitors are often more reluctant to shop around for a better deal. It's clear that organizations can't ignore the state of customers and the condition of their service experience if they expect to keep customers over the long run.

THE COST OF BAD SERVICE

If you're still not convinced that good customer service pays off big-time, then consider this. Bad service costs you big-time. In a groundbreaking study, the Genesys organization conducted one of the first global surveys on customer service. In its research findings titled "The Cost of Poor Customer Service," Genesys reported that the companies studied in 16 countries lost roughly $338.5 billion each year due to customers lost as a direct result of poor service experience.[5] While it's true that you can't please everyone, ensuring that you retain a sufficient number of customers consistently is critical to the organization because defecting, disgruntled customers *will* hurt your future business.

MAKE CUSTOMER SERVICE PROFITABLE

In order to keep customers around and increase the revenue they bring to the business, it's essential that you deliver value through products and services. But even that's not always enough. In order to remain relevant after delivering on what customers expected from you, there has to be something extra that will give customers something to talk about and a reason to continue working with your organization again and again. Your efforts to go the extra mile to keep your customers are well worth it. Once customers come to see the great value you deliver to them, they become brand ambassadors and extend your ability to reach new customers and grow the business.

Making service memorable and thus increasing the likelihood of profitability isn't hard. Some simple methods get you started:

- Make customers feel *welcome.*
- Make customers feel *comfortable.*
- Make customers feel *understood.*
- Make customers feel *important.*
- Make customers feel *appreciated.*

As a team, come together and identify ways that you can reach your customers in a more effective way. Use all of your people to brainstorm new ways to connect with customers. Not every idea has to be implemented, but ensuring that all ideas are heard will make it easier for all team members to buy in to the renewed emphasis on customers. Once you've identified your approach, ensure that all team members clearly understand their role and can consistently deliver on the expectations of customers. The change won't happen overnight, and just doing it once won't make it permanent. In order to see long-term value and profit from service, it'll take a daily effort of working to make and keep customers.

When you get the service experience right, everybody wins. Service teams win as they feel more empowered and effective for the impact they're able to make in the life of the customer. Customers win as they feel invigorated by having a service provider so determined to address and exceed their specific needs. The organizations win as they see greater value from renewed customer relationships and the impact it has on the bottom line.

Rule 51

MAKE CUSTOMER SERVICE A DAILY PRIORITY

▶ When American Express reported a study conducted showing that 78 percent of customers actually stopped doing business with a company because of a bad customer service experience, it showed that customer service isn't just a nice thing have, but is a critical business function that is nonnegotiable for organizations that want to retain customers.[1]

No business wants to lose customers. So why do so many lose business because of bad customer service? No organization actually sets out to deliver bad customer experiences, right? Obviously not. So why do they still happen? Why do customers continually get frustrated and jump from service provider to service provider, hoping to find someone that actually cares about them once the payment for services has been received?

LOSING FOCUS ON EXISTING CUSTOMERS

Most organizations aren't delusional, conniving, and scheming, or run by corporate bosses who are looking for any possible way to take advantage of customers; they just simply lose focus. In the spirit of growth and acquiring new customers and creating new business opportunities, it's too easy to lose sight of the base that got you where you are. This growing gap between the service customers expect and the experience actually delivered happens gradually, and often without the service provider realizing it. Little by little, the emphasis becomes not on servicing and retaining the customers you have, but in getting that possible new customer you want to have. The service gap happens when we lose sight of who's most important in order for great customer service and awesome customer experiences: the customer. The focus becomes instead on the strategy or the process of acquiring the potential customer. We don't set out to do it, but for one reason or another, in the pursuit of the possibilities, we find ourselves neglecting what we've been given.

The service priority problem is a real challenge that any organization can face. Rare bad service moments can be dealt with through good service recovery. Frequent bad customer service demonstrates that effective customer service management is lacking in the organization. So what's the right balance between providing excellent service to the customers you already have and acquiring new customers in order to grow your business? One possible solution lies in the three Ds of high-performance service organizations. Bain developed a service model based on research from high-achieving service organizations. These organizations used specific service models in order to ensure consistent focus on serving customers and to continually keep clients happy. They aim to *design* the right service to provide what customers need, *deliver* the exact offer customers expect, and *develop* the processes and frameworks for that to repeat without flaw.[2]

Instead of falling victim to the "It's not my problem" mentality, high-performance service organizations focus on customer needs, deliver on service brand promise, and support the system where service delivery becomes a sacred function of the organization. Customer service then isn't seen as a cost center, but an investment of doing business, and is a critical mechanism for long-term viability of the organization. The contact centers aren't viewed as a cost center, but rather a possible differentiator in the vastly competitive global marketplace.

SEEING THINGS FROM THE
CUSTOMER'S POINT OF VIEW

From start to finish, everything should be easy and enjoyable for each of your customers. If it's not, people are going to head elsewhere. And, if you think about it rationally, can you blame them? Instead of bemoaning your own bottom line and the inconveniences you're dealing with on your own end, take some time to walk a mile in your customer's shoes. Thanks to the Internet, customers have a million places to spend their money, so give them a good reason to choose you.

At DigiCert, an SSL Certificate and certificate management solutions provider for enterprises, the service team has a policy of helping both customers and noncustomers. When customers who purchased from a competitor accidentally call DigiCert for customer support, the support team members actually assist their competitors' customers. The next time that customer wants to make another purchase, you can guess what company he will turn to. There are even some online reviews by customers who started with a competitor, became frustrated by slow service and lack of communication, then turned to DigiCert to have their orders processed, delivered, and configured before the original provider responded to the initial request. That's customer service at its best.

Great service is the best policy. Effective and efficient communication is central to good customer service experiences. Communication is vital to every relationship, and the relationships with your customers are no different. So, if your supplier stood you up and it's going to take a little longer to make your deliveries, just say so. Or, if your best cake decorator is out for whatever reason and you're working round the clock to compensate for it, explain the situation up front. It's far better than making up a story that no one is going to believe anyway! Just don't confuse honest communication with making excuses. Excuses don't really mean that service has happened. Customers hate excuses almost as much as they hate bad corporate attitudes!

SHIFT FROM REACTIVE TO PROACTIVE SERVICE

In a study of business executives, roughly 80 percent believe their organizations deliver superior customer service. However, only 8 percent of customers of the same organizations believe they're getting outstanding service.[1] There's a clear disconnect between what businesses think they're doing for customers and the actual service customers want. The business world has a long history of aggressive marketing and cold-calling. As a result, many organizations are afraid to take a proactive service approach for fear of being perceived as overbearing and losing customers because of it. However, being proactive in service communication is a key customer demand that is missing from many service organizations. New approaches to service delivery and proactive communications need to be developed.

PROACTIVE COMMUNICATIONS AND CUSTOMER NURTURING

Preventative communication allows you to address a possible issue or question before it even happens. A good example of this is the team at Sage North America who routinely call their customers and business partners before the busy tax season to see how they can help. Many organizations today are turning to proactive chat to engage with customers whose behaviors don't fit the typical customer habits for a specific action, before a customer becomes frustrated with the customer experience.

At the preventative stage, your social media strategy would include monitoring the channels for any feedback or mentions left by your customers, even when they are not communicated to you directly, and engaging those clients in an easy, nonintrusive manner to see if you can help them. Ask customers to participate and voice their frustrations as well as suggestions to get an idea of how your customers see their ideal experience and work out solutions to deliver that experience to them. You could engage them through surveys and polls, ask them to vote on your next big idea, leave a comment about a new product, etc.

Nurturing service is aimed at bringing the maximum value to the customer and strengthening your relationship with them. What are the ways you could bring value? You can develop unique cross-sell and upsell offers tailored for particular customers considering purchasing history, interests, and feedback given. Every piece of customer data you have at your command can and should be used to create an offer of maximum value to them.

Effective nurturing systems should enable cross-channel, multi-channel interactions. For example, suppose a customer has filed a support ticket with you and has been exchanging emails with one of your support reps. The rep should also have an option to start a chat with the same person right from his mail application, jump on a phone call, or even reach out to the customer through social media.

SOCIAL SPOTLIGHT

Have you ever received a response from a major brand when you contacted it through a social channel? If so, you're one of the lucky ones. Most brands today are falling short of the opportunity to stand out that social channels offer. Featuring customers in your corporate social mentions or blog article features is an easy (and cheap) way to really connect in a personal way. When I wrote my first blog post about Hewlett-Packard's customer forums and the success it had had in creating a customer community, I got a few tweets from HP's flagship Twitter account. I'm still smiling about that today. Since then, I've interacted with American Express, Hallmark, Zappos, and others, leading to major positive brand connection. The cost to these organizations was minimal, yet the impact was immense and will forever change how I view these brands and their customer care teams.

Most companies still don't use social channels effectively, even though social media can give your business a competitive edge. The opportunity isn't just a shift from reactive to proactive; it's a shift from ordinary to extraordinary—from generic interactions to exceptional experiences.

GET SOCIAL AND PERSONAL
WITH CUSTOMERS

▶ With incredible technologies and new ways to not only market to customers, but also to interact with them on a personal level, why would any business not take advantage of what's available to them? I'm talking about social media, and it most certainly is everywhere. It's right under your nose with two of the most powerful outlets on the Internet: Facebook and Twitter. Companies like Zappos serve as an exceptional example of going beyond being a "company" in the eyes of their customers and becoming more of an entity, a conglomerate of people, employees who truly care about their customers and prospects. Let's look at how you can achieve the same.

GET SOCIAL

Customer service *is* social interaction. If you try to defer it to machines and automated processes in order to minimize customer interaction for the sake of improving your bottom line, or thinking that somehow it'll help your business, you're wrong. Great customer service is the backbone of a great business. Remember, you're not in the auto business, the plumbing business, the merchandising business, the technology business—you're in the *people* business, and it's time to embrace that and start making yourself known online.

USE FACEBOOK AND TWITTER
TO COMMUNICATE WITH CUSTOMERS

Stay in touch with your customers using Facebook and Twitter, communicating with them and showing them that you're not a faceless business but somebody who cares about the experience they have with you. You'll find that not only do your customers start to love you and return again and again to your business, but they'll be bringing their friends with them as well. Remember, social networking is also a form of social documentation. If you do right by a customer on Twitter or Facebook, all of their friends are most certainly going to see it as well. Even if customers don't say a word to their friends, the contact is visible to all and your commitment to their satisfaction speaks volumes in itself.

Don't be afraid to talk with your customers. Treat them like people, not just as cash cows that need milking. Believe me, they notice when you do. One of the best parts about social networking—it's free. Facebook and Twitter are free, as are forums. Lack of funds isn't an excuse, so get out there and make some customers smile. Many organizations today are stepping beyond the traditional templates of corporations and using service as a way to increase engagement with customers and develop their reputation as more than just another company. These organizations have learned to create value and support customers beyond the actual product purchase or service process. They've been able to integrate themselves into the daily workflows and conversations by interacting in a personal way beyond traditional customer service.

DON'T BUILD ANOTHER YOUTUBE—
TAKE ADVANTAGE OF IT

Define goals that clearly determine what you want to do on those contact channels and what you hope to get from engaging with customers. You don't need to build a completely new channel, just find out where your customers are, and then do something that's meaningful to them.

Marques Brownlee is a wildly popular technology reviewer on YouTube. His YouTube channel has millions of subscribers. Marques didn't set out to build an alternate video site for his technology review videos; he leveraged the existing social platform to create his special niche. A simple, focused goal has helped him connect with passionate users to achieve his exceptional success.

KEEP UP ON SOCIAL MEDIA

You can't chase every new thing, but you need to be aware of social tools available to you. If your customers are there, and there's an opportunity to add value through the channel, you should consider using it as part of your customer service efforts.

While it's more difficult for some organizations and brands to fully engage in social media, you can still work with the community as sponsors or assign dedicated team members who share similar passions as community members who add a personal face and represent your brand.

Rule 54

STOP CREATING CONFLICTS FOR CUSTOMER SERVICE

▶ Customer service can often mean very different things to the provider and to the customer, meaning that there's often a big disconnect between what the customer expects and the demands of a call center. Of course, no business intends to provide bad customer service; however, it's often the end result. So why is it so difficult to change? Through neuropsychological research, we've learned that there are two main driving forces in our minds: emotion and logic. Furthermore, it seems that these two mind powers are constantly battling it out for control over us.

THESE OPPOSING FORCES CONTROL OUTCOMES OF CUSTOMER SERVICE

Compare riding a horse with riding an elephant. In theory, the rider has control of the reins and it doesn't matter which animal he's riding. The rider sets the course and determines the best way to reach his destination. However, due to its size, riding an elephant is a lot different from riding a horse. An elephant has its own instincts and it emotionally interprets scenarios and situations along the way, often steering both animal and rider off course.

This struggle for control has been noted in customer service interactions between call center staff and customers. It's not easy to reach a state of harmony between emotion and logic, because logic is pretty straightforward, and emotion is difficult to interpret and put into practice. It's a challenge trying to get people to identify and understand the current emotional and logical climate and to use it to their advantage. You'll fail if you attempt to control every customer engagement, because you can't plan for each one and you can't preempt every service situation. In fact, you will create conflicts for customer service if you try to impose hard-and-fast rules on situations where both logic and emotion are in play.

CRAFT A FRAMEWORK INSTEAD OF CARVING POLICIES

Your aim should be to provide a framework for a workable process whereby opportunities can be taken to implement positive change, leading to great results that appeal to both companies and their customers. Because customers' emotions, objectives, problems, strengths, and challenges are often different in each case (including each interaction and with each organization), this problem demands a dynamic, flexible approach to developing positive customer relationships.

Service agents should be given the flexibility to provide responses to customers that fit the situation, offer various options, and make decisions on the spot. An angry, emotional customer doesn't want to be told that the person he's talking to doesn't have the authority to waive a late fee or send a package overnight. He wants an immediate solution, not to be passed along to someone else to explain his problem all over again. By establishing a dynamic, flexible approach to customer service, you'll be helping to eliminate conflicts, not create them.

Rule 55

BUILD A CUSTOMER EXPERIENCE WONDER OF THE WORLD

▶ Every year, organizations are spending more and more money, using more and more resources, and interrupting the life of the customer more and more. Too often, organizations try to make up for a lack of innovation and ingenuity by paying for more visibility or increased volume. Most organizations will never achieve worldwide renown. But if you're setting out to be the best pizzeria in Provo, Utah, or if you're a financial planner in Boynton Beach, do you really need to be known in Paris, London, or Shanghai? Would it make a difference to the local customers you serve?

Instead of widespread popularity, focus on establishing a reputation for persistency, efficiency, effectiveness, and responsibility. These attributes are the core of the dependability that will deliver value to your customers.

DON'T DO IT FOR MEDIA; DO IT FOR THE CUSTOMER

When the Seven Wonders of the Ancient World were completed, outside the scope of their immediate audience, they remained unknown to most of the world, although they were magnificent achievements. But did the lack of renown diminish the accomplishment? Of course not. Most of your accomplishments will never be recognized except by a few individuals, and that's OK. The ultimate service result should be to make a difference in the life of a customer.

Every company that sets out to conquer through experience is working to build its own version of a wonder of the world, at least in the eyes of its customers. Wonders aren't built overnight. They take considerable effort and attention to detail. Every component plays its part, and through the efforts of many, greatness is accomplished. You're responsible for your own persistence through the process of creating the wonder your customers will experience. It will be a learning experience, it will stretch you, and it'll be different from anything else you've previously done, but it will also be well worth the effort once it's accomplished. Have you ever come away from working with a customer questioning whether you could have done something differently to drastically change the outcome of the interaction? Was there something you could have said that would have won this customer's business for life? We often get so obsessed about the details of the *work* that we forget about the *purpose* of customer service.

Author Daniel Pink, in his book *To Sell Is Human: The Surprising Truth About Moving Others* (Riverhead Books 2012), points out that "Your job as a persuader, as a motivator, is to reset the context and surface people's own reasons for doing something. Because it works a lot better." Working together with a customer means more than just convincing the customer your product or solution is right. It's more than just making a sale, getting a customer to buy something else, or convincing them to buy again in the future.

The true nature of customer service is being concerned about how you're helping customers succeed in getting what they need. Each customer interaction needs to be put into this context in order to stay true to the purpose of service. This should always take precedence over service metrics and process workflows. It's too easy to get caught up in the mechanics of service work. However, one key question should be the foundation of every future business decision and set the stage for each customer interaction: How does this decision contribute to the success of the customer? This question should help frame the strategic approach of the service agent and help in the decision-making process of service work.

HELP THE CUSTOMER BE SUCCESSFUL

Focusing on the success of the customer immediately propels you beyond the trap of simply selling a product or reciting talking points of services offered. As you focus on how you can contribute to the success of the individuals you service, it shows true empathy and the desire to see them do their best. Business decisions then aren't related to the number of units or the price of a product, but to the effect of the solution on the life of the customer. This is at the heart of organizations that are truly customer-centric.

When you focus on the success of the individuals you serve, the motivating factor for the customer to use a product or service isn't that you've said the right words or pushed hard enough, but that it's in the customer's own self-interest to do so. Asking the right questions helps change your frame of reference from being about you and instead puts the customer first. How does your customer do X? Why do they do it that way? How do they find what they're looking for? How do they go about making a decision? What factors do they consider in making a decision? What ultimately is the deciding factor in their choice of service?

Simply selling to customers is the model of the past. Connecting with and engaging with customers in a positive way today requires that you think of yourself as an advocate on behalf of the customer.

STAY RELEVANT

There's a wise saying in business that says that *if you don't like change, you're going to like irrelevance even less.* As a prime example of the customer-experience revolution, Amazon has shown the way to innovate and dominate by putting the needs of customers first. Making experience the heart of business strategy, Amazon has shown that customer service and customer experience really do matter and are critical to staying relevant to today's Internet-savvy, socially connected customers.

The focus today is quickly surpassing the product or the price and emphasizing the purpose of the customer experience itself. We're seeing that it's easier and easier today to imitate a product or service. But service is difficult to duplicate and execute at masterly level unless you have total buy-in to customer focus. Innovate a product, and your competitors can quickly catch up. But innovate on experience and you can quickly leave the competition behind forever. Delivering exceptional customer service is critical to ongoing success today. Customer needs have changed, and those who want to remain relevant will need to continually keep up with the wants of customers. You can build your own Wonder of the World for your customer.

Rule 56

TRAIN EVEN WHEN THERE'S NO TIME TO TRAIN

▶ Spending four to six weeks putting a new customer service agent through training is a lot of time, and it can quickly cost you a lot of money. When you hire a new employee, you need to know right away, not weeks later, that the person is serious about the position. Here's how you find out, and how you start training your customer service agents when you don't have that kind of time and money to invest in unproductive training.

You can't put a fresh customer service agent in position and expect her to perform without some semblance of training. Expecting the person to produce positive results like a well-trained team member would be completely unreasonable. Instead, give her a bit of training on her first day—something small, a minor responsibility to start doing that will save other agents time so they can focus on more productive tasks suited to their experience and skill set.

This will show the newcomer's willingness to learn and take on tasks. As new hires start getting familiar with their tasks, introduce more bits of training, so they can take on an additional responsibility. This approach is actually very powerful, because it helps new customer service representatives acclimate to the job more comfortably. This way, they end up completing helpful tasks that contribute to your overall business, and they're doing it from day one.

TRAINING MATERIAL

Experience is the greatest teacher, but your customer service and call center agents are still going to need some time and material to understand what it is they need to do in order to succeed in their position. So where do you find this time? How about between tasks, or if they're already taking calls, between calls? Why not set an hour after their lunch for them to watch training videos and screencasts?

HANDS-ON EXPERIENCE

When you teach your employees a little bit, and then have them immediately put that training to use, you help that training solidify in their minds much more quickly than if they had to go through a long, extensive course without any field training or experience. As the boss—or as a manager—communicate with your new customer service agents to make sure they understand the subject matter of their training. Ask them questions, and, in turn, answer any questions they have. Lead by example, and treat them as you would want them to treat your customers. All of this maximizes training, experience, growth, job satisfaction, and employee retention.

Don't expect the new people to be star customer service agents right from the start. If they are, that's great! Chances are, though, they'll need steady on-the-job training, discipline, and experience. Be a good boss and build good employees in the process. They'll stick around, learn what you need them to learn, be good to your customers, and bring in more money for the company.

If you want to continue to deliver the type of experience that customers care about, it takes more than just solving customer problems today. You have to look to what customers experience today and how you want them to experience working with you tomorrow; then create the foundation for training your people so they'll be able to consistently deliver the results that customers want.

Rule 57

REMEMBER THE MOST IMPORTANT TEAM BUILDING HOUR OF THE DAY: LUNCH HOUR

▶ Great workplace cultures and places where people love to work are environments where people are emotionally involved, happy, and excited to come to work. One of the keys to achieving this is getting to know each other as individuals and as part of a team. Having this type of relationship helps keep team members engaged with each other, as well as with the organization and its overall goals.

Blogger and New York City–based programmer Joel Spolsky points out on his blog the importance of the lunch hour and the positive effect it can have on the development of a team.[1] Being part of a group and fostering camaraderie by eating lunch together is vastly superior to eating by yourself at work. A simple 30- to 60-minute break away from your desk spent with others in a cafeteria or restaurant is a stress reducer and a great way to develop the sense of culture within the organization. With busy work schedules and projects, lunchtime is a critical hour when we can come together as teams and cultivate our common purpose.

Encourage your team members to take time to sit down with other people on the team or others in the organization and talk about anything and everything. This interaction will go a long way to cultivating the type of open communication and familiarity that makes people more effective in working together on their assigned projects. The greater the level of familiarity between members of a team, the greater will be the ability of the individuals to work together to accomplish the mission of the organization.

PROMOTE INTERACTION ACROSS
THE ORGANIZATION

Successful organizations will often provide free or inexpensive lunch for its employees. The benefit of having individuals gather together at lunchtime far outweighs the cost of the food being provided. These organizations know that food at work is not just a perk to be checked off as a requirement for companies today. They recognize that having this type of atmosphere develops the type of employee relationships needed for an organization to succeed.

Associating with other individuals in your organization should be nonnegotiable. Make it a requirement that team members cannot eat lunch at their desk, except for extenuating circumstances. Organizations can go even a step further, developing interdepartmental relationships and collaborations by asking their people to sometimes eat lunch with others outside of their immediate group. Does this mean assigned seating at lunch? No, but encouraging teams to open a spot or two at the table for someone they don't know or inviting a group from another team out to lunch helps to break down the traditional barriers between people and teams across the various departments in our organizations.

DO NOT EXEMPT MANAGEMENT

Management team members also should make sure to interact with others both at lunch and during the workday. They can and should take it upon themselves to visit various groups on a regular basis and work with them in order to create a more personal relationship with different teams. For smaller offices, simply setting up shop with a group temporarily for a day or two, or even a week at a time, can do this. For larger organizations or global teams, this might mean quarterly or semi-annual visits need to be scheduled. There's a cost associated with those visits, but an even higher cost to the organization for relationships neglected that result in inefficiencies, poor communication, or lack of collaboration.

PROVIDE A REAL SERVICE TO YOUR CUSTOMERS

▶ A few years ago, I had the enlightening opportunity to have Don Gallegos come speak to our company here in Utah about developing a customer service culture. Customer service in America is weak at best, since great customer service is missing at so many organizations. It doesn't have to be this way. Don wrote a book titled *Win the Customer, Not the Argument* (Raphel Marketing 2005), which is the best customer service book I've ever read. At the heart of this eye-opening book is the topic of *what is great customer service?* What do your customers define as great customer service? How does your organization deliver great customer service?

YOUR CUSTOMER CARES ABOUT GREAT CUSTOMER SERVICE

I've made *Win the Customer, Not the Argument* the only required reading for employees at work. Great customer service means navigating through the potential problems of doing business while delivering an exceptional customer service experience. You can avoid a poor customer experience by creating a customer-focused culture with:

- Great customer service quotes
- Great customer service stories
- Great customer service examples
- Great customer service skills trainings

All of these are excellent sources of inspiration for any team that wants to set itself apart from the competition and deliver great customer service.

DITCH THE DUMB CUSTOMER SERVICE RULES

Why do companies sometimes establish new policies that annoy or anger 90 percent of their customers? Don't they know that you have to take care of your 90 percent customer base or they'll go elsewhere? Dumb customer service rules and pointless, useless policies are some of the main sources of frustration and disappointment for customers today. Unfortunately, it's not only your customers who suffer, but your employees, too. They'll struggle to deal with the amount of red tape and dumb rules in place that prevent good *customer service* from happening with each customer interaction. People hate pointless rules and policies that don't make sense. They anger customers, and they destroy employee morale when you force people to just do it because "that's the way it has always been done."

QUESTION EVERYTHING YOUR TEAM DOES

Every task, function, and assignment that is currently being done needs to be reviewed and evaluated. Our team improved our efficiencies and turnaround times to our customers by 50 percent in nine months by simply dropping some tasks that didn't really matter to our customers and offered little or no value to the ultimate customer experience.

ELIMINATE ALL TASKS, POLICIES, AND PROCEDURES THAT ARE REDUNDANT

Companies often get stuck with operating procedures that make for redundant tasks. Look at what you're trying to accomplish and cut out everything that is already being done somewhere else. If certain portions of work are repetitive, use macros, hotkeys, shortcuts, and auto features to make work slicker, quicker, and more efficient. Reuse work as much as possible.

TAKE CONTROL OF YOUR OWN PRODUCTIVITY

The way too many of us work today sucks—to put it bluntly. It's time we take control over our own productivity and stop sitting around blaming others or waiting for someone to do something about it. You are in control, and it's time for you to start looking around at the time wasters and inefficiencies holding you back from achieving results. Stop serving the customer relationship management (CRM) system at work and start serving customers.

The burdensome rituals and outdated processes of yesterday's way of doing business are shackles to creativity and innovation that prevent individuals from truly exercising their ability to connect with the people they serve. Sure, every organization needs structure and processes, but have you ever heard of a customer who publicly praised corporate policy? Instead of quietly allowing the day-to-day repetition of work to drain the emotion out of doing your work, decide instead to take control and create your own system for success that delivers value and personal return on your work investment.

IDENTIFY WHAT GREAT CUSTOMER SERVICE IS

Here are a few suggestions for offering *real* great customer service, not the customer disservice that we're currently receiving from the corporate giants:

- ▸ If your phone system message always says that you are "experiencing an unusually high volume of calls," it's not really unusually high unless you're the IRS and it's April 15. Either hire more people or get rid of the message; it's insulting to your customers.
- ▸ Actually respond, and respond quickly, to emails and chats. Give customers the attention that is needed to resolve the problem as soon as possible.
- ▸ Requiring a receipt for a return is ludicrous. You have complex systems for tracking inventory, stocking, pricing, serials, and so on. Why should a customer need to prove that the item came from you by showing you a receipt?

▶ If someone didn't need to show a driver's license to buy it, why does he need it for a return? Don't ask for one.

▶ When a customer is frustrated over chat or just isn't getting it, sometimes it helps to give her a phone call.

▶ Don't feel handcuffed by policies. If a customer wants a refund after 40 days (10 days past the 30-day refund deadline), just give it to him.

▶ If a customer is upset, forget the policies. Give her a full refund. Give her something extra. Keep her happy in the long run.

▶ If a customer is angry that the product doesn't work like he thought it would (even if it is a known incompatibility), replace it—or better yet, give him a new product that works—for free.

▶ If a customer goes out of her way to write an email and thank you, send her a package with something free.

USE GREAT SERVICE TO CREATE
CUSTOMER LOYALTY

Winning customer loyalty centers on the idea that your customers are not just customers from the moment they walk in the door to your business or visit your website, and so on. They are customers 24 hours a day, 365 days a year. They are always customers. Companies have started to treat people as onetime customers and not as lifelong customers. People are loyal to themselves first. If you don't take care of them, they will go elsewhere. Your excellent customer service is the greatest answer your customers can give to a competitor trying to steal them away.

Remember these principles, from previous rules:

▶ People don't know great customer service until they get it. When they receive good service, they think, "Wow!" and make the choice to switch to the new service provider.

▶ Customers are not always right, but they are *always* customers.

▶ Don't take the easy way out and say no; find a way to say yes.

▶ Don't hide behind a policy; do what's right.

▸ If 90 percent of your customers are good compared with those that are bad, why create policies that hurt those good customers?

▸ Just because you make a special situation for one person, doesn't mean that everyone else will want that same thing! Make each customer happy.

Nordstrom's once took back a pair of tires and refunded the customer's money. Nordstrom's doesn't even sell tires. Nordstrom's won that customer.

Bad customer service doesn't have to be the standard. You have to make it your mission to deliver great customer service that creates an exceptional customer experience.

DON'T JUST ANSWER THE PHONE; DO THE RIGHT THING

▶ Al White, creator of the Zen of Customer Service blog, once shared an experience he had that illustrates companies with poor customer service vision. Al ordered a promotional "free" item and was subsequently charged by the service provider. After going through the lengthy runaround process of having the service provider find the charges and arguing with multiple levels of managers, he was finally able to have the charges reversed. What kind of impression did that leave for the future? Will he ever trust that provider again?

I often wonder what kind of conditions people in customer service are working in that creates circumstances where customers are constantly frustrated and have to fight to get the service they need. Why do companies have to make it so difficult for their customers? It's as if they really don't want you to be their customer.

Al White's story points out the fact that customer service people need to have the freedom to do the right thing. And then they need to go out there and do it. In this case, everyone failed. The company failed, the employee failed, and the customer service supervisor failed.

Instead of forcing customers to fight to get an incorrect charge reversed, could the agent have simply said, *"I can't believe that! That's not right. Let me refund it for you right now. Can I offer an extra month of service to make up for the hassle?"* Problem solved, customer saved. Instead of fighting with customers, show customers you work for them; then do whatever it takes to make things right for the customer. Set the following ground rules for exceptional customer results:

- ▶ Agree with the customer; it diffuses the upset customer.
- ▶ Whatever was done wrong, fix it.
- ▶ Acknowledge your customer's hassle.
- ▶ Offer something to make up for it.
- ▶ After finishing with the customer, let the manager know about the issue. There will probably be other people who might encounter this same situation, and you'd hate to be creating more angry customers.

TAKE A BREAK, WANDER AROUND, AND HAVE SOME FUN

I confess that I goof around in the office quite a bit. I sometimes take random timeouts to have Nerf gun fights with different team members in the office. OK, maybe it's not just sometimes; it's frequently. I've been known to pull out blankets and have a team picnic for lunch in the middle of the office. We've had spontaneous videogame tournaments, in-office touch football games, golf-putting challenges with boxes and other random office items for obstacles, movie nights in the conference room, and many more random activities.

There's a reason why I chat about sports and other nonwork topics, go out to lunch with different team members, and shoot Nerf guns with my customer service team. These things release some of the tension and break up the routine we get into each day. Because we have a young workforce, these activities liven up the mood in the office and help people relax. Ultimately, the fun and games unite the different teams and improve our moods, which affects our customer service delivery and the actual service our customers receive. In order to amaze your customers, you must provide consistent service performance. Relaxed, refreshed, happy team members are essential to achieving that consistency.

BREAK UP THE ROUTINE

Depending on the type of business you conduct, the activities your people perform will differ greatly. Nevertheless, it's critical that you do something to shake off the monotony of day-to-day work. Yes, there's always something new happening and lots of work to do. But for most professionals, each day means answering the same question they've answered thousands of times for other customers in the past. Without some way to break up the repetition of service work, it's easy for people to fall into a rut, and ruts lead to stale service or even edgy attitudes. And while you help team members unwind, you'll also often find a vast trove of information that will better help you gauge the morale among team members and the conditions on the front lines of customer service.

GET POSITIVE RESULTS FROM
YOUR WANDER-AROUND TIME

When organization managers and leaders wander around and interact with team members, the group benefits from the social relationships that are developed. Wander-around time is about getting real face time with team members, uniting them as a team, and rallying them around the customer-focused mission of the team. During this wandering time, stop to listen to people and get their thoughts and feelings on how their work is going, how their life is going, how the team is doing, what their challenges are, what can be done to make the overall employee experience at work better, and what can be done to make the overall customer experience better.

Breaking the monotony of everyday work doesn't need an agenda. There's more to it than just getting status updates from the team, and training meetings don't count. It's about interacting with people in a personal way and creating time for the informal contact that strengthens personal relationships within the team. Casual interactions work best when they're frequent, friendly, positive, and unscheduled. Otherwise they seem fake, and that's detrimental to the atmosphere of the office. The first few times you try to initiate casual interactions, you might get a good deal of hesitation from those present, or even somewhat mixed results. Don't stop; don't use that as an excuse to give up. Try other break-the-monotony activities. Eventually, you'll find out what works best for your group.

Here are a few tips on how to get the best results from your wander-around time:

- Be unpredictable with your contacts (it can't be a daily 10 a.m. walk-around).
- Ask questions and *listen* to what people have to say. *Do something about it!*
- Make personal connections with team members. Talk about *non-work* items.
- Seek out *all* team members. Don't just gravitate to the most social, or the ones you get along with best.
- Do it often!

BE A FORCE FOR CHANGE

▶ Creating service policies is easy. The challenge is developing the frameworks to implement them and having them adopted across your organization. New service initiatives are often difficult transition periods. What do you do when you've come up with a great way to improve your organization, but you don't have the authority to change company policy? The process may seem daunting, and it can be overwhelming at times, but any individual in an organization can be the force for change in instilling a new vision and a new way to connect with customers. Creating and maintaining the type of change that transforms the organization doesn't begin in the boardroom; it begins in the hearts and minds of the employees on the front line.

So how do you begin to influence the business to make a change you truly believe in? You first have to think about what customers need and how your organization can address the needs of customers. You then have to identify the most effective ways to deliver on those needs in a way that exceeds customer expectations and creates positive value for the business. Finally, it's critical for you yourself to continually perform and do those actions consistently. Don't wait for others; take it upon yourself to start the process of change. Many people have initiated great changes by making a simple decision to start taking action. Where you are now is less important than recognizing the opportunities around you. Even if you lack the experience or skill, resources are available everywhere today for you to learn, practice, and become an expert at what you want to achieve.

BE BOLD AND LIVE BY EXAMPLE

Few employees are bold enough to go against the grain. What's there to lose if you commit to making a stand? Are you afraid for your job, for your paycheck? Those concerns tend to scare people into submission, but if your idea for policy change is truly a good one, then it will almost certainly be in harmony with how the organization currently conducts business.

Policy is in place for a reason, and usually that reason is because it works. If you can show that your policy works even better than the old one through practice and example, then you're positioning yourself to have maximum leverage in legitimately changing the current company policy to the one you're advocating.

YOUR CONVICTION WILL SHINE THROUGH

Fortune favors the bold and punishes the halfhearted. You have to be serious about the change you want to incorporate. It's human nature to desire to blend in and do like everyone else. But going the extra mile and passionately delivering the change you want to see will— over time—take hold across the organization. If the example you're setting starts to make a positive difference in the service experience, you'll notice that customers come to your business, eager to see *you*, eager to do business with *you*, and remembering *you*.

So long as your change is truly beneficial to the company, and so long as you persist in being the living demonstration of it, it will grow until the positive effects are undeniable to the people who do have the power to officially change company policy. When the company takes up the change you desire, don't rush to claim the credit. Allow it to take life and transform you and your organization as you work to serve your customers.

As you change yourself, your changes will affect others around you. As they change, too, change will continue to roll on. As you change how you think, you will change how you feel. As you begin to see things in a different light around you, you'll also begin to act in ways you never would before. Even with the decision to change, there will still be moments of confusion, frustration, and disappointment. Realize that it's all part of the growing, learning, and process of living.

The true effect of change isn't always seen immediately following the decision to change. Change requires simmering as old habits break down and new possibilities are infused into the building blocks of the new actions taking place. Be patient through the process, and enjoy the experience of being a positive force for change.

KEEP YOUR CUSTOMER RELATIONSHIPS FRESH

▶ It's challenging to keep customer service relationships fresh, so I've put together some strategies to ensure that long-standing customer service relationships are always fresh and never grow old. Managing effective customer relationships requires the right combination of understanding your customers, delivering the right experience for each customer, continually attracting new customers, increasing profitability for the organization, and decreasing customer management costs. Keeping your customers happy and your business thriving is challenging, but it's not impossible. Rather than work in the dark, always fearing that customers will turn away or never show up, there are some basic experience touch points that every organization can implement in order to continually refresh the relationship with their customers. These small steps can easily be overlooked, but they make a major impact on how customer service is perceived and contribute to an exceptional customer experience.

KEEP YOUR CUSTOMERS INVOLVED

It's a great idea to ask your customers what business issues are worrying them. This is a thoughtful touch, which shows that you care about them as individuals. And, by gaining a little bit of information about their concerns, you may be able to help resolve their problems. Customer relationships are built on customer service. Each and every word, action, and behavior in customer service proves to your customers the value you are placing on them.

ASK FOR CUSTOMER FEEDBACK

Impressive customer service requires a good understanding of your customer. Everyone is different. Asking for and receiving useful and frequent feedback from your customer will greatly assist in crafting your customer service ideals to best suit and ultimately impress your customer. Ask yourself on a regular basis what you can do to make your customers be efficient and effective. Perhaps you won't have anything to offer most of the time, but once in a while you may be able to suggest ideas that just may help with their jobs and careers. This shows your genuine concern for their personal welfare and for their business careers.

DON'T FORGET THE PERSONAL TOUCH

Customer service is the easiest place to connect with customers. Encourage your team members to use their initiative in following up with customers and letting them know that you actually do care about them. *"Thank you for your business"* notes are always appreciated. An appropriate time for these could be on each anniversary of your first business dealing together. Other ideas are to send out holiday cards, or have thank-you tokens in your retail store to show customers your grateful appreciation.

SHARE PERTINENT AND INTERESTING INFORMATION

Nothing motivates a CEO more than beating the competition to the punch. You can help with this by sharing breaking news on competitors with your customers. Your direct customer service report looks really good if it's filled with competitive information and news, prior to the customer's CEO knowing about it. This could include pertinent industry information or information relating to a specific service or product. Your customer can then offer this information to the CEO and look incredibly efficient and strategic in the process.

LEARN FIRSTHAND ABOUT
THE CUSTOMER'S BUSINESS

Have you ever considered spending some time (perhaps a day) with a customer or his sales team? Your customer could only be delighted to think that an outsider is prepared to invest precious time to learn more about their business. This may not lead to anything, other than you now know your customer and his business a lot better, but it might just provide enough information for you to be able make some useful suggestions. Either way, your customers are going to be appreciative and impressed.

CONDUCT INTERNAL ACCOUNT AUDITS

You must ensure you're working continuously for your existing customers, and that they know it. Consistently hold regular internal account audits and invite employees who *are not* working on the customer's business to review what you're doing to confirm that the work being done is in the best interest of the customer. Give these outside voices the ability to use their experience and insight to suggest alternative approaches to working with the customer. Oftentimes, their fresh point of view can uncover unique and effective ideas for developing the customer relationship and other times nothing at all. I always make sure the customer knows we're investing additional time in thinking through creative solutions to their business challenges.

MASTER THE ART AND SCIENCE OF CUSTOMER EXPERIENCE

▶ Human behavior and how people interact is a science because humans feel and react certain ways to stimuli, like anything else living on this planet. The art of customer service is in understanding and learning to deliver the stimuli that create favorable long-term results. Mastering the art and science of customer experience requires you to learn to carefully balance the use of words as part of your service actions. This requires an understanding of those winning words and phrases that can influence each customer situation, and also an understanding of the workflows, processes, and decisive actions that will ultimately deliver the service that customers remember. Getting this right is at the core of the customer *wow* factor.

The *wow* factor is powerfully effective. To deliver it, you have to think outside the box, using your imagination and innovative thinking to do whatever it takes, even if it's unorthodox. You must create your own style that differentiates you from all other services. Your customer service has to be exceptional enough to win that customer back, time and time again. The *wow* factor is the customer support driver.

THE SCIENCE OF CUSTOMER SERVICE

Professor Noriaki Kano, a lecturer and consultant specializing in quality management, developed the customer satisfaction model known as the Kano model. The Kano model studies service programs that are proven to succeed and the ways in which the customer service teams in these programs work together to meet the needs of the customer. Kano recommends specifically focusing on three main areas that, when applied to customer service experience, include:

1. The basic requirements of customer interactions
2. The service differentiators
3. The constant inspirational reminders that keep service on track

Kano believes that by concentrating on these three areas instead of trying to guess what the customer wants, the customer's needs will be fully met and this will effectively encourage returning loyal customers (long-term).

The Basics
Basics include positive actions, tone of voice, choice of words, and providing an easily accessible, reliable means of contacting the company. Without these basics in place, you will instantly create dissatisfaction with your customers. Satisfaction is not delivered merely by having the basics in place, but it's the foundation that allows the potential for developing and delivering a *wow* experience factor in the customer service.

The Differentiators
Differentiators go beyond predictability and giving customers what they really need. They have the power to deliver a truly exciting customer experience. This excitement comes from the unexpected delivery of something positively memorable, a service that is delivered like no others, producing something that gives the customers more than their expectations (the element of surprise). This would work in any service industry niche.

The Constants
The constants include having the desire to drive a high performance that consistently provides a satisfying customer experience. A low performance factor achieves dissatisfaction, and these distinguishable

factors need to be fully understood. Performance in its entirety is linear and symmetrical when it comes to customer satisfaction. You have to strive to become competitive, to establish a connection with the customer via relationship building that will allow you to explicitly and effectively understand the customer's needs.

THE ART OF CUSTOMER SERVICE

Customer service is also an art form because you're negotiating with behavior and emotion, using both verbal and nonverbal communication skills that require having the ability to interpret and communicate effectively, using your imagination. All situations are unique, each one presenting different problems that need innovative solutions. It takes a creative mind, skill, and experience to handle each situation successfully. We focus on all these aspects and creating environments through our own style of communication, to enhance the customer's positive emotions. This is what it takes to provide the customers with a memorable exceptional experience—to get to the *wow* factor. Their long-term loyalty cannot be won or encouraged as effectively in any other way.

We're all individuals, and for any one of us to become content with how we are treated in any given scenario, someone else has to be sensitive enough to pick up on our immediate needs through observation and imagination. That someone would have to be able to relate to other people and be sensitive to their needs—someone who has a unique talent for reading situations well and who can instinctively act decisively.

If customer services are delivered robotically as if there are always regimented correct procedural answers or questions in a customer service interrogation, then customers are unlikely to return to that same dehumanizing experience again. On the other hand, if customers are ever pleasantly surprised by the way you've treated them, they are likely to advertise those pleasant new experiences accordingly by word of mouth.

Rule 64

OPTIMIZE YOUR DIGITAL EXPERIENCE

We live in an age of great technological advancement. What are you doing to optimize the online customer experience? Too often, we think of *customer experience* as a personal conversation with customers or a pleasant-looking store or polite employees. We place too little concern on the popular, preferred medium of business of today, the Internet, and this neglect leads to a poor digital online customer experience. Envisioning the experience your customers have when they interact with your business is an important step in developing customer-facing policies that generate positive real-world experiences. But considering the full range of touch points available in the digital marketplace, this critical task is definitely not getting any easier.

> *As Internet–connected devices spread and people adopt them, companies can reach and engage with their customers wherever they are and in new ways not possible through brick-and-mortar stores, television advertising, and catalogs.*[1]
>
> —JOHN R. RYMER, VP AT FORRESTER

Rymer predicts that companies will need to accommodate as many as 10 additional customer service touch points in the coming years. This means that business leaders must overcome challenges to stay focused on business goals and avoid getting dazzled and distracted by every new tool that comes along for customer engagement. To remain focused and effective, marketing pros need to stay grounded and commit to platforms that are most meaningful to their target customers.

Is your service delivering technology that contributes to your customers' positive experience? One of the common problems with online marketing and advertising is that businesses spend vast amounts of money on online advertising, search engine optimization, and marketing campaigns to attract customers, but these online marketing campaigns do little to contribute to the actual customer experience.

YOUR WEBSITE IS A REAL COMPONENT
IN THE CUSTOMER EXPERIENCE

Don't overlook the importance of your website to the customer experience. And I'm not talking about adding movies, intro videos, flashing lights, sounds, or things that pop out of the screen. Those are distractions and gimmicks from the early days of the web. I'm not looking to watch a movie online (I have Netflix for that). I just want to contact your company or buy something, so don't make me sit through your intro video and don't make me dig through your site to contact you.

Customers ultimately really only want three things when working with a business online:

1. Fast
2. Cheap (fair price/value)
3. Nice atmosphere with help, if needed

When the customer is taken to a website that is not optimized for the online customer experience, it defeats the purpose of all of the advertising you've done and all of the work to build your brand into something memorable, and you miss the opportunity to make a positive, lasting connection with your customer. If the advertising or marketing campaign outshines the image of your website, then you've already lost the battle in getting customers and creating future loyal customers. They are left feeling disappointed with the final result and may feel they've been misled.

$$$$$ FOR MARKETING,
$ FOR CUSTOMER EXPERIENCE

In reality, it's not a matter of making customer experience spending equal to marketing spending; I don't think that's realistic, or necessary. But an optimized experience has to be part of the plan. You have to give real consideration to the online process and how you will create a seamless delivery from the presales to the sales process through post-sales and product or service support. Customers need to feel like it's all part of one unified business plan. I want to focus on some ways to optimize this process for digital experience of your products and services.

LOOK AT THE COMPETITION'S
ONLINE PRESENCE

Your customer experience doesn't have to be as good as Apple; you just have to beat your competitors. When focusing on the overall customer experience, one easy way to figure out where you are and where you need to improve is to first look at what your competitors are doing and work on becoming better. Learn what customers in your industry are looking for: Why do they choose competitors over you? What can you learn from the way your competitors do business? How can you make a difference to give you the advantage? You'll be amazed at what you can actually learn from a competitor when you change your focus from reactive thinking to proactive thinking.

APPEAL TO YOUR CUSTOMERS' FEELINGS

Customer experience is about the feelings they have when visiting your website. The use of videos, music, sounds, and images in motion is becoming a common feature of websites, but don't get sucked into that. To avoid simply filling a website with endless amounts of text, some companies try to stimulate the senses with all sorts of bells and whistles. But it's not the senses you want to engage, it's the feelings customers get when working with your brand. Focus on making your website professional, useful, functional, straightforward, useful, clean looking, functional, and useful (did I mention that already?). The easier, faster, and more useful your website is for customers, the better the feelings you'll develop within customers. Those good feelings then will be associated with your product or service and your brand.

HONESTLY ASSESS YOUR WEBSITE

Many companies are too careless with the customer experience. They don't realize how important the little things really are to the overall experience. We've all heard the saying, "Don't sweat the small stuff." It's true for many things, but not for the customer experience. We carefully craft marketing language and create welcoming places of business; we train our people to be polite, professional, and helpful. We typically go out of our way to please our customers. Sometimes, though, we get lost in our processes and forget some of the small things that can quickly add up to frustrate our customers. Take a minute and look over your website; ask complete strangers to give you honest feedback. Take the time to optimize your website or system to maximize positive potential for an exceptional customer experience.

TECHNOLOGY SHOULD ENHANCE THE EXPERIENCE

Pew Research Center's Internet & American Life Project reports that more than 90 percent of American adults now have a cell phone, with 58 percent of adults owning a smartphone.[2] Smartphone ownership and usage continue to grow as the availability and cost of new technologies continue to decrease. Suppose your company sells gardening supplies in a bustling neighborhood and relies on attracting business from homeowners throughout the city. Build an informative website for a home-based computer, but also invest in a meaningful mobile website design containing a few pages of the most critical information, such as your physical address, hours of operation, and a mapping feature that provides directions to the store. From there, offer your customers a branded app that helps them manage seasonal plantings for your climate zone or provides some other relevant utility.

Too many service providers miss opportunities for better customer engagement online. Today's consumers are mostly Internet savvy and can navigate their way around a website, blog, or social media site with relative ease. It's possible to win customers without speaking to them at all. People enjoy solving their own problems if the path to the solution is simple and straightforward. As long as contact information is easy to find and phone operators are always available to help with more complex problems, the website additions discussed in this chapter can certainly increase customer service satisfaction.

ALIGN YOUR DIGITAL EXPERIENCE
WITH PERSONAL SERVICE

When it comes down to it, automated website pages, forums, social media sites, and virtual assistants can only do so much to satisfy the needs of your customers and clients. The hands-off aspects of winning customer service can make the process smoother and less cumbersome for both consumer and company, but to really win the customer into being a loyal lifetime customer, personal attention is needed when they have a complaint or other issue.

The key is to focus on the simple questions that help you understand your customers, their needs, and the value that you can offer them to separate yourself from the hundreds and even thousands of other organizations out there doing the same thing you do. Getting digital right means being able to relate to a new generation of customers, taking into account their specific demands and preferences, then overcoming the current technology gaps in the marketplace and taking advantage of opportunities that your competitors have created for you to get and keep customers. By aligning your digital and face-to-face branding efforts with customer habits and preferences, you can demonstrate a high level of understanding and respect for the people you're targeting for business. This kind of effort makes customers happy, and that leads to better business overall.

GET TO KNOW A NEW CUSTOMER EVERY DAY

▶ Being comfortable is nice, it's pleasant—and it's also the bane of entrepreneurial progress. When you're too comfortable, you don't strive, you don't grow, and you don't achieve new heights in your business. You begin to rely on regular customers you're familiar with and your business tends to generate an average profit month after month, sustained by those who most commonly frequent your business. What causes so many businesses to just reach a certain point and start coasting? It's comfort and familiarity, which certainly sound wonderful and in short bursts can even be very healthy, but to a company that sets out to be outstandingly successful, it's like slow poison. What can you do to overcome the creeping embrace of comfort? Simple. Get to know a new customer every day.

AVOID THE PAIN OF COMFORT

Comfort in business is typically born from consistent repeat customers, from your regulars. Who doesn't want that, right? However, there seems to be an invisible ceiling, where the company is easily self-sufficient and you're earning enough money to be happy. What got you to that point? Customers, of course! You've had to go through the process of marketing and convincing prospects to become paying customers, so why stop? You've done the hard part, you've built the momentum, and so to coast now would be a serious mistake. All you've got to do to avoid this is get to know one new customer per day. That's it. Train your customer service agents to learn names, to make follow-up calls, to turn a stranger into a friend. This small daily commitment will help to ensure that your business thrives while others of similar nature struggle and go under.

SHOW CUSTOMERS YOU CARE

Who cares about how customers feel? Pretty much no one. And they're starving for that kind of attention. No matter what kind of business you run, you can fulfill this burning need. Almost 70 percent of customers leave a company because they perceive that the company is indifferent to them.[1] They feel that they have no value in the eyes of the business, so they abandon ship and take their money somewhere else. All you have to do is convince a prospect or customer that you care. This can't be faked, so your concern for them must be genuine, and that means having genuine employees as well. Here are just a few simple things you could do to solidify your customer relationships, as well as turn new prospects into devoted regular customers:

▸ Get to know your customers on a first-name basis.
▸ Remember customer preferences and ask about them on their next visit.
▸ If they've made an appointment, greet them when they come in, and show that you've remembered exactly why they're visiting.
▸ As they leave, thank them for their business; remember to again use their first name.

These are just a few examples, but the similarities should be clear. Remembering a person's name, why they're at your business, and other things they say—all of it shows that you care, and it establishes a strong bond. This bond is not one of business and customer; this is the same kind of bond that forms between friends. Get to know just one new customer each day. Learn customers' names, ask about them, and memorize what they tell you. This gesture will make a world of difference for your business, and your consistently growing profits will reflect your commitment.

START EVERY NEW EMPLOYEE IN CUSTOMER SERVICE

▶ Delivering excellent customer service isn't just the duty of select employees that you dub "customer service agents," but of all staff under your employ. Your business is your life, and fantastic customer service is like your armor. When you have holes in your customer service, when some employees are delivering a positive customer service experience while others aren't, you have some heavy chinks in your armor, and it *will* cost you. I'm sure you've had the experience of speaking with somebody working in a grocery store—perhaps someone stocking shelves. You ask this person to help you locate something, and he either doesn't know how to help you, or is so impersonal, or both, that you walk away shaking your head, feeling a little annoyed and unhelped.

How does this affect your perception of the company or business? Certainly not in a good way. You probably don't think to yourself, "That employee isn't responsible for providing customer service, so it's fine that he wasn't able to help me." Nope, instead you naturally feel that it's a reflection on the business. You'll bury that experience in your subconscious so that whenever you think of that company, your feelings will be affected by the negative experience you had with its untrained, impersonal employee.

Customer service is so critical for your business that it cannot be understated. Some people say that marketing is the Holy Grail of a business, and maybe it is, but you can bet that when people buy from your company, aren't satisfied, and then have a lousy customer service experience—they're going to be very vocal about it. They're going to tell all their friends and make as much of a fuss as possible. Believe me, no amount of marketing is going to bring back a customer you could have saved if only you had better customer service. So what are you supposed to do?

PROVIDE CUSTOMER SERVICE
TRAINING FOR EVERYONE

When I say everyone, I mean *everyone*, because it only takes one untrained and unfriendly person in your employ to botch a relationship between a customer and your business.

- The shelf stockers—teach them customer service.
- The IT tech people—teach them customer service.
- The marketing designers—teach them customer service.
- The janitors—teach them customer service.

Companies try desperately to present an "image" to a customer, the goal being to present the business itself as an entity. This is often called *branding*. If you want to maintain a strong brand, then your entire staff must work in harmony when dealing in customer service. If you fail to do this, you run the risk of your company coming off as being two-faced. People do not want to give their money to what they perceive to be a dishonest business.

MAKE CUSTOMER SERVICE YOUR MISSION

There are businesses that thrive and flourish on customer service alone, while others sink below the waves of mediocrity, because they rely on gimmicks and marketing to try to stay afloat. There's no substitute for exceptional customer service. When every one of your employees *exudes* the desire and ability to serve customers in an exceptional way, the people who frequent your business will be able to tell, even without speaking to every individual employee. All you have to do is make customer service training mandatory. No matter what role employees will fill, be sure to run them through appropriate customer service training. The friendly custodian or helpful IT guy could be the difference between a onetime customer and a lifetime customer. They transform your business in the eyes of your customers, making you, and your brand, seem less like a business and more like a friend.

ALLOW FOR RANDOM
ACTS OF WOW

▶ To win the customer means you must be exceptional. We've been through this already, but I'll say it again—people are used to being treated poorly by businesses. If you're able to surprise someone with an unexpected positive experience, and even more powerful, a positive *wow* experience, you're likely to find that person becomes a customer for life. The key word here is *unexpected*.

Fortunately for you (and this may sound a bit jaded), the bar is set pretty low. Customers expect to be treated like faceless numbers, which is why the thought of having to dial up a customer service line or fill out a support ticket causes anxiety for the average person. This has become a learned response, and that's where your opportunity exists to really wow your customers.

PROVIDE SERVICE LIKE THE BEST OF THEM

The Ritz-Carlton Hotel chain gives its hotel staff members $2,000 each, just in case they need it to make things right for a customer, no questions asked. How unusual is this? How outstanding is it compared with any other business? If you visited a business and anything went wrong or was not to your satisfaction, would you expect a customer service agent of some sort to be standing by with $2,000 in cash, ready to do whatever it takes to make it right for you, to make you a lifetime customer? No, it would be a complete surprise to you!

You too can be like this. (I don't mean you have to give each employee $2,000 to handle customer service problems!) You can position your business to surprise and wow your customers, even in a seemingly random way. You can offer this to your customers without spending tons of cash. In fact, there are ways you can do it with very little extra cost. Imagine scenarios like these:

- An IT company spontaneously giving a client a free month of service.
- A cash gift card and a warm, handwritten letter sent to a recent client.
- A custom-made recording or video of yourself, thanking that customer personally for their recent business and continued business in the future.

Yes, yes, you can do things like send them coupons to give them a discount on their next visit. This is pleasant, but it's nothing that will wow your customers. When they receive a handwritten letter and a token of appreciation, it will wow them and definitely leave a lasting impression that will keep them coming back to your business time and time again. Going the extra mile in customer service is a prerequisite to giving customers the wow moments you're trying to instill. Zappos once had a customer who really wanted to talk, so the service agent stayed on the phone with the customer and talked. The call lasted over nine hours! Do you think that customer was surprised? Do you think she's going to come back to Zappos every time she needs shoes? You bet she is!

Seize your opportunity. It's not hard, and it only takes a little bit of creativity and cash to make a huge impact on customers, enough of one to keep them coming back to your business time and time again. Give it a try, be a bit spontaneous, and show your customers some random acts of *wow*. Don't be surprised when they come back again.

GET A REALITY CHECK

▶ Service leaders are the individuals ultimately responsible for orchestrating the entire service workflow for the organization. They are lauded when the organization earns profits or applause, but the same people are criticized when the organization does not achieve its goals. This is why service leaders are always walking the tightrope. If your organization is failing in meeting targets, increasing performance, or is having problems with staff retention, then it is time for you to carry out some introspection by giving yourself a reality check.

While carrying out the introspection, the first question you should try to answer is, Why were you given the role of a leader in the first place? There were some positive traits in your character that inspired senior management to appoint you as a service leader. These are your key strengths, which can decay with time. If you feel that you have moved away from certain positives, then try to bring them back again. Apart from this, ask yourself these pertinent questions.

ARE YOU REALLY INSPIRING OTHERS?

If you are not positive mentally, you can never inspire your team to attain great heights. The words and attitude you use when you're in a confident state should work like magic on the underperforming staff. Check your levels of commitment, loyalty, motivation, and performance. If the organization is not moving in the right direction, are you responsible for it in some way? If you are running low on motivation, commitment, loyalty, or any other aspect, go talk to someone who holds a senior position. You need a coach to see you through this phase. Any weakness in your leadership will be noticed eventually by management, so do not hesitate in seeking help.

You must address your shortcoming before the employees start to feel it. If the employees spot your weakness, then the work philosophy of the team will go down.

What were the positive aspects of your best boss? While climbing up the ladder, you must have worked under various bosses. There are probably some whom you would prefer to forget, but there must be one you consider the best boss you ever had—maybe even "the perfect boss." Try to think of what made the person so good as a boss. What were the strengths of the person? You'll find that the person had some of the following positive attributes:

- He believed in the strengths of his employees.
- She was readily approachable.
- He always had time to listen to employee problems one-to-one.
- She asked for opinions, ideas, and inputs from all employees.
- He was strict but treated everyone fairly.
- She did not have ego or control issues; she put the organization and its employees over everything else.
- He was honest and open. If some of your requests were denied, the boss explained why they were not accepted.
- She treated everyone within the team equally, no matter what their designation or role.
- He was a good teacher who trained you using questions, not by giving lengthy lectures.
- She was very sociable and friendly, though professional.

ARE PEOPLE GOING THE EXTRA MILE?

Everyone has a reserve of energy. Some of your employees choose to use that extra energy, while others just like to cruise through the day. Yes, staying in safe mode protects the employee from any major mistakes, but it's not ideal for the organization. A great leader is capable of getting that 20 percent extra effort from the team members. So, judge whether your team is giving that extra effort regularly, with perhaps occasional days of safe working.

ARE YOU PROVIDING REAL FEEDBACK?

Employees look to their leaders for feedback. Whether it is positive or negative feedback, it helps an employee grow and improve. If an employee has achieved something remarkable, go public with your praises. This will give the employee a boost in self-confidence. Negative feedback can be equally important, but it should be given in a private, one-on-one conversation. Negative feedback should be given after careful analysis.

Remember, you are the mentor of team members, and it is your responsibility to help the employees grow with creative inputs. Whether you lead a team for big data analytics services or a contact center, this introspective expedition should bring out the positives in you. You'll feel rejuvenated and confident in leading the team. This will help you get back to top form as a leader and help your organization attain its short-term and long-term goals.

CREATE CUSTOMER EXPERIENCE DISRUPTION

▶ All businesses that want to continue growing and prospering must keep informed and up-to-date with customers' changing needs and wants. For any business looking for the perfect example of how customer experience has become its own revolution, look no further than Amazon. Amazon has shown the right way to dominate and innovate by putting the needs of its customers first. An extraordinary customer experience is at the heart of Amazon's business strategy. Amazon believes that a customer's experience is what's most important and is the secret to staying relevant to today's socially connected and Internet-smart customer. Amazon has completely changed the customer experience.

Today, doing business really means providing the perfect customer experience. Organizations are quickly discovering that the words *customer service* are not just words to throw around. Yes, customer service is a strategy, but it's also the only real way to conduct business today, and it's the only way to get and retain loyal customers. It seems that this is a lesson already learned by Amazon. What follows are some of the simple yet effective Amazon methods of providing an exceptional customer experience.

MAKE IT EASY FOR CUSTOMERS

Amazon is a web-based business, focusing on providing customers with a journey that's as straightforward as can be. Its checkout process is quick and simple with the creation of their One Click shopping; customers no longer have to reenter their credit card details every time they make a purchase.

Customer service has also been expedited for those who have a query or wish to return an item. Information is automated and readily available by the use of self-service tools, supported by email and web chat.

SHARING EXPERIENCES

Amazon's exceptional platform for real customer reviews is central to its online shopping experience. Most Amazon shoppers use reviews for trusted advice when considering making any purchase on Amazon. Today, almost all retailers offer the opportunity to review products and experiences; certainly most online shoppers wouldn't make large purchases without first checking reviews of the retailer and the products concerned.

PREEMPT WHAT YOUR CUSTOMERS NEED

The Internet has been responsible for the completely different way we shop today. Before, our choice was rather limited, but now we have so much choice, it can be overwhelming. Amazon created the "Frequently Bought Together" concept, whereby when you purchase an item Amazon will automatically show you what other customers purchased with that same product.

If, for example, you're considering the purchase of a Blu-ray player on Amazon, you'll see the suggestion of purchasing the HDMI cables to go with it. This is a win–win situation for both the seller and the buyer. The purchaser has the opportunity to buy something they may not have thought was sold on Amazon, or perhaps didn't realize it was needed, and of course the seller sells more product. Where this concept is really worth its weight in gold is when toys are being sold without batteries or other necessities.

With its huge amount of captured data, Amazon is able to use it to provide personalized recommendations and offers, based on your previous purchase history. This ensures that your shopping experience is tailor-made just for you.

NEVER STOP EXPANDING
AND INNOVATING

In the beginning, Amazon was perceived as solely an online book-store, but this was never Amazon's ultimate goal. It was merely a starting point on which to encourage shoppers to have confidence in purchasing online. Of course, since that time Amazon has expanded way beyond retail, providing digital downloads, streaming services, and physical products such as the Fire Tablet, the Kindle E-Reader, and the new Fire Phone. Amazon is always moving forward, never resting, always searching for ways to provide the ultimate customer experience.

IT'S ALL ABOUT YOUR CUSTOMERS

We understand that, compared with competitors operating physical stores, Amazon functions on a very low margin. Amazon has always been focused on customers over competitors, looking at the long term over the short term. The rumor mill has it that Amazon's core retail business only just breaks even, with overall profits very small compared with its total revenues. I'm not recommending that you copy that business plan, but you can certainly emulate Amazon's customer-centric focus.

THE STRENGTH OF AMAZON

Amazon has the ability to think as a customer would, and to provide what the customer wants—and more. This creates loyalty in what is a very crowded market, because customers feel safe and secure shopping in the Amazon environment. Consumer behavior has changed a lot over the past 20 years with a widening choice for consumers and a shifting of balance of power between customers and businesses.

Amazon was there at the beginning of this customer service revolution, and it's still very much at the heart of it. It continues to reshape how we shop, and it seems that Amazon will also be leading us into the way of shopping in the future.

Rule 70

STOP MAKING RESOLUTIONS; START MAKING SERVICE BETTER TODAY

▶ Instead of grandiose and glamorous lists of dramatic changes that you want to make, think instead of one simple thing you can stop or start doing right away. Don't resolve to lose weight; resolve to go to the gym today. Then repeat. Don't resolve to transform your organization into a customer service machine; simply resolve to make a difference for one customer today. Then repeat.

Starting something new, developing a new habit, or cutting something out from what's going on already is hard. But then again, we're talking about actually achieving something and it's not supposed to be easy; otherwise we wouldn't be talking about this. Cutting back and reorganizing your goals takes self-awareness, self-discipline, and emotional intelligence.

IMITATE THE PEOPLE WITH PASSION

There's something about getting so caught up in the checklist approach that it really is just checking tasks off a list, nothing more, and nothing is really getting accomplished. At the end of the day you can look back and see your to-do lists completed, but be completely devoid of emotion. Those who truly get what customer service is all about and understand the importance of creating a wonderful customer experience know that it's not the to-dos but the why-dos that really matter.

Do you ever notice how successful and prosperous the most generous people tend to be? I'm speaking of the people who you always see smiling, who always radiate wealth, goodwill, and happiness. You ask them what they do and they'll tell you all about their business that they built from the ground up, and all the wonderful people they get to help because of it. This is what I'm talking about.

These people believe in themselves and they believe in others. They seek to make the world a better place, not just through their wonderful and uplifting attitude, but through every aspect of their business as well. This is the kind of person you can be, and the kind of business you should be seeking to build—one that makes the world a better place.

KNOW YOUR OWN PASSION AND LIVE BY EXAMPLE

In the military, an upstanding squad of men is a reflection of the captain or commander in charge. Your business is similar, in that it is a reflection of you, at least in the eyes of your customers. You don't have to be selfless in order to make the world a better place. After all, businesses are meant to generate income, to secure profit, and to desire more income for yourself and the people you love is not a bad or harmful act. Everybody wants to take care of the people closest to them. All of that said, it's time to look at what your business does and to be completely honest with yourself in the process, and to do this, you must first take a hard look at yourself.

What Is Your Interest?

What drives you? What makes you feel like you are accomplishing something?

- Take more than you give.
- Charge the most while giving the bare minimum.
- Find out all the corners you can cut in your business.
- Beat out the competition.

What Is Your Philosophy?

What is your guiding principle? If you had to put a slogan on your life, what would it be?

‣ Get money, get paid.
‣ I'm the boss and I know what's best.
‣ If we can't fix it, it's their problem, not ours.
‣ Get in, make money, get out.

You'll notice that all these ideologies have a negative slant, but that's how some people believe businesses grow and become successful—by having a stern and competitive mindset and doing "what others don't have the stomach to do." This isn't the case, as you can lift up people's spirits, feel fantastic about the service you're providing, and still run a successful, profitable organization.

When business owners are so focused on how to maximize profits at any cost, they almost invariably do so at the expense of their own staff and customers. The gains may come, but they will be temporary. Instead, focus on maximizing the positive experience your customers have at your business. If it costs a bit more, so what? You'll make up for it tenfold over the months and years to come.

Don't be shortsighted; don't get caught up in chasing the money. Focus your business on making the world a better place for your customers, and I promise you will—in turn—be making the world a better place for yourself.

Notes

RULE 2 ▶ CREATE THE RIGHT CULTURE FOR SERVICE

1. Google, "Our Culture," http://www.google.com/about/company/facts/culture/ (accessed March 1, 2014).
2. Jamie Notter, "Definition of Organizational Culture," http://jamienotter.com/2013/05/definition-of-organizational-culture/(accessed August 15, 2014).

RULE 3 ▶ LEARN HOW TO UPDATE YOUR CUSTOMER

1. Scott Edinger, "Three Elements of Great Communication, According to Aristotle," *Harvard Business Review* (January 17, 2013).

RULE 4 ▶ SERVE PEOPLE, NOT SHAREHOLDERS

1. Francesco Guerrera, "Welch Rues Short-Term Profit 'Obsession,'" *Financial Times* (March 12, 2009). Accessed March 12, 2009.
2. Yasser Ahmad Bhatti and Marc Ventresca, "The Emerging Market for Frugal Innovation: Fad, Fashion, or Fit?" *SSRN Electronic Journal* (March 15, 2014).
3. Dawn House, "Utah's Harmons Celebrates 80 Years of Reinvention," *Salt Lake Tribune* (August 3, 2012). Accessed April 10, 2014.

RULE 5 ▶ PUT THE RIGHT PEOPLE IN THE RIGHT PLACE AT THE RIGHT TIME DOING THE RIGHT THING

1. James Allen, Frederick F. Reichheld, Barney Hamilton, and Rob Markey, *Closing the Delivery Gap* (Bain & Company, 2005), http://www.bain.com/Images/BB_Closing_delivery_gap.pdf (accessed February 8, 2014).

RULE 10 ▸ FIND A WAY TO SAY YES EVEN WHEN THE ANSWER IS NO

1. American Express, "Good Service Is Good Business: American Consumers Willing to Spend More with Companies That Get Service Right, According to American Express Survey," press release (May 3, 2011), http://about.americanexpress.com/news/pr/2011/csbar.aspx (accessed July 20, 2014).

RULE 16 ▸ MICROMANAGE EVERY DAY

1. MEJ Newman, "Power Laws, Pareto Distributions, and Zipf's Law," *Contemporary Physics* 46, no. 5 (Sep/Oct 2005): 323–351.
2. See 80/20 Rule, Pareto Law, and Pareto Principle at 80-20pre sentationrule.com. http://www.80-20presentationrule.com/whatisrule .html (accessed August 10, 2014).
3. Lerzan Aksoy, Timothy L. Keiningham, and Terry G. Vavra, "Nearly Everything You Know About Loyalty Is Wrong," *Marketing News* (October 1, 2005).

RULE 29 ▸ BE LOVABLE TO YOUR CUSTOMERS

1. Jeffrey Kluger, "They're Alive! Why Apple Products Are Irresistible," *Time* (October 7, 2011).

RULE 34 ▸ CHANGE HOW YOU THINK ABOUT CUSTOMER SERVICE

1. *2011 Customer Experience Impact Report* (Oracle, 2012), http://www.oracle.com/us/products/applications/cust-exp-impact-report-epss-1560493.pdf.

RULE 35 ▸ REALLY GET TO KNOW YOUR CUSTOMERS

1. Kate Leggett, "Understand Communication Channel Needs to Craft Your Customer Service Strategy," Forrester Research, Inc. (March 11, 2013).
2. *2011 Customer Experience Impact Report* (Oracle, 2012), http://www

.oracle.com/us/products/applications/cust-exp-impact-report-epss-1560493.pdf.

RULE 40 ▸ CUSTOMER EXPERIENCE IS MORE IMPORTANT THAN ADVERTISING

1. Tanya Irwin, "Study: Spend Ad Money on Better Buyer Experience," MediaPost, March 24, 2011 (Accessed September 20, 2014).
2. Ibid.

RULE 44 ▸ LEARN HOW TO EARN YOUR CUSTOMER'S LOYALTY

1. William Boulding, Ajay Kalra, and Richard Staelin, "The Quality Double Whammy," *Marketing Service* 18, no. 4 (1999): 463–484.

RULE 50 ▸ FOCUS ON THE VALUE OF GREAT SERVICE EXPERIENCE

1. Natalie Petouhoff et al., "The Economic Necessity of Customer Service," *Forrester* (January 21, 2009), p. 2.
2. Ibid.
3. Frederick Reichheld and Phil Schefter, "E-Loyalty: Your Secret Weapon on the Web," *Harvard Business Review* (July 1, 2000).
4. "Service Trumps Price, Verint-Sponsored Research Reveals," *Contact Centre Live!* (November 21, 2012).
5. Genesys, "The Cost of Poor Customer Service," Alcatel-Lucent Company (October 1, 2009).

RULE 51 ▸ MAKE CUSTOMER SERVICE A DAILY PRIORITY

1. American Express, "Good Service Is Good Business: American Consumers Willing to Spend More with Companies That Get Service Right, According to American Express Survey," press release (May 3, 2011), http://about.americanexpress.com/news/pr/2011/csbar.aspx (accessed May 9, 2014).
2. James Allen, Frederick F. Reichheld, Barney Hamilton, and Rob

Markey, *Closing the Delivery Gap* (Bain & Company, 2005), http://www.bain.com/Images/BB_Closing_delivery_gap.pdf (accessed February 8, 2014).

RULE 52 ▸ SHIFT FROM REACTIVE TO PROACTIVE SERVICE

1. James Allen, Frederick F. Reichheld, Barney Hamilton, and Rob Markey, *Closing the Delivery Gap* (Bain & Company, 2005), http://www.bain.com/Images/BB_Closing_delivery_gap.pdf (accessed February 8, 2014).

RULE 57 ▸ REMEMBER THE MOST IMPORTANT TEAM BUILDING HOUR OF THE DAY: LUNCH HOUR

1. Joel Spolsky, "Lunch," Joel on Software, April 28, 2011. Accessed April 10, 2014. http://www.joelonsoftware.com/items/2011/04/28.html.

RULE 64 ▸ OPTIMIZE YOUR DIGITAL EXPERIENCE

1. John R. Rymer, "The Future of Digital Customer Experience Is More Than Mobile," John R. Rymer's Blog, August 28, 2012. Accessed October 10, 2014. http://blogs.forrester.com/john_r_rymer/12-08-28-the_future_of_digital_customer_experience_is_more_than_mobile.
2. "Mobile Technology Fact Sheet," Pew Research Centers Internet & American Life Project (January 1, 2014).

RULE 65 ▸ GET TO KNOW A NEW CUSTOMER EVERY DAY

1. Karen Klein, "Building Customer Relations by Listening," *Businessweek* (June 1, 2007).

Index